The Work of Nonviolence

Readers are encouraged to go to www.MissionPointPress.com
to contact the author or to find information on how to buy this
book in bulk at a discounted rate.

MISSION POINT PRESS

Published by Mission Point Press
2554 Chandler Rd.
Traverse City, MI 49696
(231) 421-9513
www.MissionPointPress.com

Cover photo by Petra Daher, dahervideo@yahoo.com

ISBN: 978-1-950659-49-4
Library of Congress Control Number: 2020905819

Printed in the United States of America

# The Work
## of Nonviolence

## Stories from the Frontline

## Julie Thomas-Beckett

*For peacefulness,*
*Julie Thomas-*
*Beckett*

**MISSION POINT PRESS**

*For Peter in gratitude*
*for the work of his generation,*
*and for*
*Aaron and Elizabeth*
*with hope for the potential*
*in their generation.*

# TABLE OF CONTENTS

# PROLOGUE

They had come to listen to the Grand Wizard of the Ku Klux Klan at a rally in Ann Arbor, Michigan, in 1998. It was a warm spring day, so she wore a halter top and shorts to the event, while her boyfriend donned a confederate flag headband to compliment his swastika shirt. Tensions had been rising in the city as the event drew nearer...they felt it and they wanted to be part of it. As they arrived, they noticed the chain link fence surrounding City Hall. There was a stage set on the steps of the building where they could see the hooded members of the Ku Klux Klan as they stood to speak at microphones. The swell of people everywhere was exciting and oppressive at the same time.

Walking through the crowd, she noticed handwritten signs, touting "White Power" and "Go back to Africa" and "Gay sinners go to hell." There were also signs saying, "We are one human family," and "Love wins." Nearing the fence, the tension intensified as protesters were chanting and yelling over the speakers at the podium, so it was hard to hear what the Grand Wizard was saying. She watched as her boyfriend removed his leather jacket revealing the swastika on his shirt, posturing toward the protesters. He was yelling and reacting to the crowd, and then the pushing started. He shoved and was shoved in return. Back and forth it went and the attention on him grew. Then there was a bottle crashing onto his head and he was bleeding.

Suddenly, three people in yellow vests with the words "PEACE TEAM" written across the front surrounded her boyfriend and separated him from the crowd of protesters. Leading him away from the fence, she felt enveloped by the people in the yellow vests as they escorted them through the protesters. As they left the throngs of people and got to the edge of the crowd, she heard the black woman in the yellow vest say they were from the Meta Peace Team, a group that uses tactics to de-escalate violence. They were invited here today by the City of Ann Arbor to be a presence during this emotionally charged day and help keep people safe as they voiced their opinions. They led her boyfriend to a tent where there was first aid available and the three vested people started cleaning his wound, dressing it with a white gauze bandage.

When they had finished with the bandage, the man in the yellow vest turned to her and the boyfriend and said, "I would like you to know that a black woman, an Asian American woman, and a self-proclaimed 'queer Jew boy' saved your life today. It is our hope that if we ever came to your neighborhood, we would be treated with the same respect and care we showed you today."

The woman stared as the words sank into her, the pressing crowds and the signs and the heat swam in her head. She looked up at her boyfriend, and the three people with their yellow vests and said, "I guess we all bleed the same."

# INTRODUCTION

*Congress shall make no law respecting an establishment of religion, or prohibiting the free exercise thereof; or abridging the freedom of speech, or of the press; or the right of the people peaceably to assemble, and to petition the government for a redress of grievances.* [1]

As the First Amendment to the Constitution establishes, the citizens of the United States are allowed to believe what we believe, worship how we want to worship, speak what we want to say, write what we want to write, gather to share ideas and thoughts and beliefs, and petition our government with the concerns we may have about how we are governed. There are many countries across the world where none of this is possible. The people who founded our country came from places where these rights were not allowed, and they established a government where these rights were explicit. Still today, there are people who want to immigrate to the United States in search of a place where they can worship, speak, write, and assemble freely without the risk of imprisonment, torture, or even death.

Perhaps the founders had images of a utopia in mind as they wrote the documents birthing this nation. Surely, they could imagine how difficult it would be to realize the freedoms so yearned. How daring of them! Yet, here they are the freedom of religion, the freedom of speech, the freedom of the press, and the freedom to assemble that constitute our First Amendment. It is the primary list of what makes America a special place, what some would call great. In writing these into the Bill of Rights, there was an ideal set forth toward which to strive, a pole star guiding our way as a country. Full attainment of these rights without strife is the utopian aspect of the amendment. It is a tall order and one of our biggest challenges as a nation.

If we as citizens of the United States believe in the First Amendment, we need to allow people to believe and practice a religion different from our own, not demanding one religion as better than any others. As individuals, as a nation, and as a government, we need to allow people to speak their ideas even when we disagree with them. We must allow a free press to inform the people, even when the press sheds light on things difficult to see. As citizens, we must stay connected to each other, assemble in a peaceable way to communicate to each other and to those in power what ideals we hope to attain and what changes we hope to enact. This is difficult, however, when persecution and wars are started in the name of religion, when hate speech is free speech, too, when the press is labeled "fake news" or bought by moneyed interests with their own agendas, and when protests turn vitriolic and violent. This is the push and pull of America.

It is in this place where nonviolence groups like the Meta Peace Team are born. They developed out of that place of tension, and call us to rise above our basic primal tendencies, to align with others in our shared humanity. If we let ourselves.

This tension played out on July 31, 1996, a hazy summer day in Ann Arbor, Michigan, when seventeen members of the Knights of the Ku Klux Klan assembled on the grounds of City Hall to exercise their right to free speech, dressed in their white hooded robes.

The city had granted their permit and installed a chain link fence to buffer the speakers from those protesting their appearance. Black people, brown people, white people, gay, lesbian and queer people had gathered to counter the message of white supremacy with signs and statements of diversity, unity, and peace. One among them was Keshia Thomas, an 18-year-old African American woman, who, years later, reflected on the memory.

*"You never know what change can happen in just a moment. Whether you do the right thing or the wrong thing, change happens in just a moment."* [2]

In the crowd of counter-protesters was a middle-aged white man named Albert McKeel Jr. He wore a confederate flag T-shirt, and had a SS tattoo on his arm. When he was spotted, someone with a megaphone called him out, "There's a Klansman in the crowd!" Mob mentality took over and the protesters started taunting him, kicking and hitting him with their placards and signs. The man fell to the ground and the kicking intensified. Keshia Thomas saw this and realized that if things continued this man might be killed. She lunged forward and crouched over the man, holding out her arm to protect him, shielding him from the beating. An iconic photograph of the scene was captured by Mark Brunner and named one of *Life* magazine's best photos of 1996. Brunner was interviewed years later and noted:

*"I still look back at those images and wonder how things would have turned out for that man and the rest of us if she hadn't stepped in. What image would I have photographed then? Thanks to Keshia, I'll never know."* [3]

McKeel was escorted safely away, but for the scrapes, bruises and cuts sustained from the beating. He never contacted Keshia Thomas. Thomas noted that once in a local coffee shop, a teenage boy came up to her and thanked her for saving his dad's life. She realized this man who had such vile hatred for people like her-self, had a family and a life much like her own. Of her actions, she reflected:

*The incident wasn't about me. I just happened to be a vessel that carried this message. This story is about humanity.* [4]

The people of Ann Arbor, Michigan, experienced the best and the worst of humanity with this event. The rally in 1996 was fraught with tension, with some groups calling for people to shut down the speakers by any means necessary, and some faith communities instructing members to stay away altogether. The day of the rally, there were rocks thrown and windows broken. The wife of the Grand Imperial Wizard was actually struck by a thrown rock, essentially shutting down the event. The KKK vowed to return.

The community learned a lot about itself that day. It learned human beings are capable of allowing their lowest and most primal tendencies to rule the day. It also learned human beings can allow their highest nature to prevail. John Fowles in his book, *The Aristos*, notes:

*... that mankind can be split into two clearly defined groups, a Few that is excellent and a Many that is despicable, is idiotic. I say that the dividing line between the Few and the Many must run through each individual, not between individuals. In short, none of us are wholly perfect, and none wholly imperfect.* [5]

There is no "us" and no "them." We all have the ability to be good and evil; the dividing line is not between us, but within us. It is a choice of which muscle we flex.

Given the frenzy of the crowd and the violent group-think, the outcome could have been very different for Albert McKeel Jr. if not for Keshia's choice to position herself between the man and the violent crowd. She didn't know this was a technique known as inter-positioning, which is a Third-Party Nonviolent Intervention used by peace teams across the world. But the inextricable human connection she shared with McKeel, despite their vast differences, changed the dynamics of that day.

Organizers then started working together in earnest to prepare for the next rally. They reached out to the targeted groups; black people, Jewish people, gay and lesbian people. Many of the faith community got together and brainstormed on ways to counter the KKK rally. They invited the Meta Peace Team, a peace and justice group from Lansing, Michigan, to do workshops and trainings for the skills of nonviolence. For months before the next rally, there were workshops held every Saturday and Sunday for Active Nonviolence skills training. By the time of the next rally, there was a large and skilled peace coalition ready for the event. The community was prepared.

The next Ku Klux Klan rally in Ann Arbor was held on May 9, 1998, an unseasonably warm spring day. This same day at Wheeler Park, six blocks away, counter-protesters held an alternative event called CommUnity and Justice Rally, where support was celebrated for targeted and marginalized groups. Among the people at the KKK rally were 109 trained peace team members as well as the handful of so-called white supremacist provocateurs for the crowd. A space on the steps of City Hall had been set aside for the members of the Ku Klux Klan to stand and speak. Around them was a chicken wire and Plexiglas cage to protect them from thrown objects. Farther out, was an eight-foot-high chain link fence. The space between the fence and the cage was designated a "free speech area," where people could carry whatever signs they wanted and get close enough to the speakers to look them in the eye. To enter the free speech area, one had to pass through a metal detector.

Pressure was building at the fence as protesters pushed against the barriers, urged onward by the bullhorns of those trying to shut down the Ku Klux Klan "by any means necessary," including violence. As the shoving and tensions increased, it seemed the protesters were determined to create mayhem by tearing down the fence. Members of the Meta Peace Team made a consensus decision to try to maintain the fence, knowing that if the fence came down it would give the police cause to call it a riot and use tear gas or other forms of violence. MPT members, wearing their bright yellow Peace Team vests, leaned against the fence trying to hold back the growing crowd. The press of human bodies was suffocating. For more than fifteen minutes, members of the Peace Team were kicked in the groin, bruised, and shouted at, but they held the line. At one point, a young man commented about MPT member Mary Ellen Jeffreys, a thin 64-year-old white woman working at the fence. "I can't push her! She's like my grandmother." Then he joined forces with the peace team.

Despite being outnumbered four-to-one, the peace team held the fence until a few police stepped forward and used pepper spray to disperse the crowd. Once the spray settled, visible to all was the line of armed police standing four yards behind the peace team with helmets, Plexiglass shields, nightsticks and gas masks in full riot gear. It became obvious what could have happened if the Peace Team had failed and the crowd had breached the fence. Later, city officials credited the yellow-vested Meta Peace Team for preventing a riot. There were no major injuries and no arrests that day. The chief of police stood at the conference podium later that day to report on the event and said, "Usually my favorite color is blue, but today, my favorite color is yellow."

My own experience with the potential for violence occurred while attending the Women's March in Washington, D.C., in January 2017. Over a million women and their allies marched in our nation's capital that day, and millions of others joined them in cities all over the world. It was a day to celebrate and hope for a time when all people could come together as valued parts of our human family. Where we can meet at the intersections and be civil to one another, despite the different roads that bring us to that intersection. There were people of all colors, all creeds, all sexual orientations, and all economic statuses.

At Women's Marches throughout the world, there were no incidents of violence. But with the millions of marchers and the press of bodies, it occurred to me that if counter-protesters had been present, there could have been mayhem. I knew I would attend other marches in the future and that the prospect of violence would be higher, as the friction in our country rises and the partisan and economic divide gets wider and wider. The thought was sobering.

One day at our church, I saw a flyer for Nonviolence Skills Training sponsored by the Meta Peace Team. I signed up. I was pleasantly surprised to have Reverend Peter Dougherty as the trainer because I remembered him from my days in college thirty-five years prior. He had been an activist and protester for nuclear disarmament. At the training, he told stories of the MPT actions, on the ground in international hotspots such as Bosnia, Haiti, Chiapas, and the occupied territories of Israel/Palestine. MPT deployed peace teams at the Klan rallies in Ann Arbor, at political conventions, in Flint during the water crisis, in Dearborn for Arab/American festivals, in Lansing for gay pride marches and "Right to Work for Less" protests. I sat and listened intently, knowing these stories needed to have a wider audience. Despite my very large "circle of concern," I had committed myself to staying focused on my "circle of influence." I figured this was something I could actively do: to sit down and write these stories.

The more I have come to know the work of the Meta Peace Team and witnessed the everyday people who have committed themselves to nonviolence, the more I realize nonviolence is a choice. Conflict is a natural part of our humanity, not something we can make disappear. But we have a choice in how we handle it. Too often those choices include some form of violence, either verbal, physical or emotional. Some uncomfortably choose to acquiesce with passivity, which leaves people feeling powerless, victimized, and angry, often feeding the unending cycle of violence. However, there is a third response; which takes more creativity, more courage, and ultimately yields more power. It is the response of Active Nonviolence. It is working *through* the conflict with nonviolent means in order to address the differences that divide us.

There are many tools of Active Nonviolence, including:

1.  Active Listening and Effective Communication strategies, using I-statements rather than You-statements, asking questions to clarify and identify how we can align with those with whom we disagree, and finding ways to agree to disagree.

2.  Bystander Intervention tactics, which include distracting the perpetrators, directly confronting the perpetrators, engaging the help of others to interrupt the action, and checking in with the victim after the abuse.

3.  Third Party Nonviolent Interventions, which include being a presence in a volatile area which in and of itself interrupts the abusive behavior, being an observer or witness to document the actions and reactions in the conflict, Protective Accompaniment or Unarmed Civilian Protection, and if needed, the inter-positioning of our own bodies between people in a conflict escalating to violence, which is what Keshia Thomas did.

Like many in America and across the world, I have struggled with the growing divisions we see every day, causing racial, economic, religious, and partisan tensions. I have felt the stress of seeing family and friends, avoiding any meaningful discussion because there are too many "off-limit topics." I have yearned for ways to interact humanely with people who look different, believe different and vote different than I do. This book is for anyone who can feel these tensions in our society and is looking for nonviolent ways to relate to one another. By sharing stories of the Meta Peace Team and how the tools of Active Nonviolence are used, I hope to do my part in making our future better by making our present better.

———

This book is about the work of nonviolence as told through the lens of the Meta Peace Team. In Chapter 1, Reverend Peter Dougherty tells stories of his life and how he came to be involved in civil disobedience and nonviolence, and how he and Jasiu Milanowski met and started the Meta Peace Team. Chapter 2 includes many lessons of nonviolence from Jasiu and Peter from their peace team work domestically and internationally. Chapter 3 introduces Mary Hanna, the MPT office manager, who tells stories of participating on domestic peace teams, and shares research supporting the effectiveness of nonviolence. Chapter 4 illustrates the work of MPT in schools, and with the Poor People's Campaign as experienced by teacher and activist Kim Redigan. Chapter 5 applies the work of MPT on various peace teams, as Sheri Wander works with the marginalized communities in Michigan. Chapter 6 tells stories of International peace teams within the Israeli-Palestinian conflict, as experienced by Peter Dougherty and Elliott Adams, a former Army paratrooper. Chapter 7 reflects stories from Palestine as experienced by Hanna, Redigan, and Linda Sartor, and introduces the work of Jewish Voice for Peace. Chapter 8 recounts the stories, emotions, and reflections on what the Meta Peace Team witnessed at the U.S./Mexico border. Chapter 9 brings to life the stories of everyday people who are using the skills of Active Nonviolence in their daily lives. Then we reach the Conclusion, which in many ways is a beginning.

Often, an Appendix is reserved for ancillary information, but in this book the Appendix has a detailed description of a Meta Peace Team training. It could be the place to start in order to understand the practice of Active Listening, Bystander Intervention and Third Party Nonviolent Intervention. Or it could be a place to visit between chapters to increase understanding of these tools for nonviolence.

This book in no way represents an exhaustive history of the Meta Peace Team or anyone using Active Nonviolence skills. But it hopes to tell enough of the story to understand where MPT comes from, how nonviolence works, and how these skills can be used by each of us in small and large ways. You'll read stories of everyday people, using creative, bold, and active strategies of nonviolence to create a space for disparate parties to come together and interact safely. It is a verbal snapshot of a moment in time, where we sometimes know what happened before, but often do not know what happens after the moment. The people using nonviolent strategies are not people with supernatural powers. They are women, men, priests, nuns, rabbis, parents, grandparents, students, social activists, military veterans, teachers, office workers, nurses, doctors, lawyers, professors, teenagers, ministers, and everything in between. They have chosen to focus on that part of them where peace is possible. It is a choice we are all called to make as illustrated in this oft-told fable:

> One evening, an old Cherokee told his grandson about a debate that goes on inside people. He said:
>
> "My son, the battle is between two wolves inside us all. One is Evil. It is anger, envy, jealousy, sorrow, regret, greed, arrogance, self-pity, guilt, resentment, inferiority, lies, false pride, superiority and ego. The other is Good. It is joy, peace, love, hope, serenity, humility, kindness, benevolence, empathy, generosity, truth, compassion and faith."

*The grandson thought about it for a minute and then asked his grandfather, "Which wolf wins?"*

*The old Cherokee simply replied, "The one you feed."* (6)

Co-founders of the Meta Peace Team: Rev. C. Peter Dougherty and Jasiu Milanowski

## CHAPTER ONE

# PEACEFUL WARRIORS

*We must accept finite disappointment but never lose
infinite hope. —Martin Luther King Jr.*

In November 2009, the Reverend C. Peter Dougherty stepped off the plane in Mumbai, India, and was greeted by the warmth of a gentle ocean breeze. While he made his way through the throngs of people and the congestion of inner-city traffic, he was greeted by a distinct aroma of incense, cook fires, and strange foods. And there were smells that were not entirely pleasant.

Reverend Dougherty almost didn't get to go to Mumbai, given that his visa request had been held up. He later learned that his history of civil disobedience and resulting jail time had placed him on a list, which slowed the processing of his application. He was still without a visa, waiting to board his flight in Detroit, Michigan, before the visa was hand-delivered to him by fellow traveler Karen Donahue, a nun with the Sisters of Mercy. Shrikumar Poddar, a generous supporter of Dougherty and his work, had been able to work with the United States and Indian governments to obtain the needed clearance.

Dougherty was to receive the Gandhi International Award for his work as a peace activist and for co-founding the Michigan Peace Team. Each year, the Jamnalal Bajaj Foundation honors three people from India and one non-Indian for fostering Gandhian values, community service and social development. Bajaj was a humanitarian, philanthropist, social reformer and close colleague of Mahatma Gandhi in the struggle for independence, using nonviolent strategies to achieve their goals. He worked side by side with Gandhi and espoused the nonviolent tactics for real change in India. Years after Bajaj's death, his grandchildren created the foundation in his name, which honors people working for nonviolent societal change. As the recipient of the foundation's International Award, Dougherty accepted the honor on behalf of the entire Michigan Peace Team. Promoting Gandhian values by providing trainings in the skills of active nonviolence and placing peace teams in areas of potential conflict, MPT was proud of the recognition for Peter, who had spent his entire adult life working for peace.

Sitting in the front row awaiting the award, Dougherty visited with fellow award recipient Shri Lavanam, the son of Gora, who was a renowned atheist contemporary of Gandhi and a great inspiration to MPT co-founder Jasiu Milanowski. Dougherty and Lavanam spoke of the philosophies of Gandhi and Gora and their approach to spirituality; God is Truth or Truth is God. How serendipitous to be sitting by the son of an architect for the Gandhian peace movement while anticipating an award for his own peace work.

As the ceremony unfolded, each recipient was called to the stage by Rahul Bajaj, the patriarch of the Jamnalal Bajaj Foundation. In introducing Dougherty, Rahul said:

*He is a Catholic priest, peace activist and specialist in nonviolence. His peace and justice work began in 1970 when he witnessed campus movements against the Vietnam War and American policies of military intervention. Over the years, he co-founded organizations against nuclear weapons including Covenant for Peace, Great Lakes Life Community, and Michi-*

*gan Faith and Resistance. In 1993, Father Dougherty and others formed the Michigan Peace Team, known as MPT. Since 1995, MPT has placed violence-reducing teams in the violent occupied territories of Palestine. Palestinians say that this does reduce violence committed by the Israeli soldiers. In 1996-1998, MPT sent violence-reduction teams to Mexico, where Mayan indigenous people were being persecuted by the Mexican military and paramilitary death squads. At a racist Ku Klux Klan rally, MPT placed a team of 109 peace team members. The chief of police later praised the peace team, relieved that the violence was greatly reduced from what was expected. Nonviolent violence-reduction peace teams are the direct result of Mahatma Gandhi's vision of Shanti Sena; the 'Peace Army' of MPT embodies that vision and its creation was inspired by it. Father Dougherty is an outstanding person committed to a peaceful and just world. Over the years he has gone to jail several times, he has risked his life in war and conflict zones. In the United States, he is known as the conscience keeper, of the foremost Gandhians.* [1]

Like the other recipients of the Gandhi awards, Dougherty received a standing ovation and a golden trophy signifying people linked in a circle. He was accompanied by a small cadre of MPT supporters who had made the trip, including Shrikumar Poddar, Karen Donahue, Bob Alexander, and Julie Horn-Alexander. The reception was jovial as people celebrated the work done by the recipients for the people of India, and in Dougherty's case, for the people of the world.

Dougherty spent three weeks traveling the country on the itinerary mapped out by his Indian American friend, Shrikumar. They visited the Gandhi Center in Mumbai and spoke to many groups about the work of the Michigan Peace Team and Active Nonviolence in peace teams across the world. He visited six villages of great poverty in Bengal and went to the ashram Wardha, where

3

Gandhi lived and was eventually assassinated. As he took the train to New Delhi and Bengal, Dougherty saw people struggling to survive, desperately seeking justice for themselves. An illustration of great contradictions, India is the seat of a long and rich history with the Hindu and Buddhist traditions and spirituality. Yet, there is the presence of absolute poverty with so many thousands of homeless and handicapped people on the streets that their extreme station becomes ordinary and unseen. He felt humbled while witnessing the struggles of people economically and socially, still choosing nonviolent means to communicate their needs.

As he traveled from place to place, Dougherty spoke of the power of nonviolence. It is vital to understand how systemic violence works and to develop strategies to undermine that system. We are called upon to transform the system, to tear down the patterns of oppression, to build new systems of peace and justice with more equitable ways of inter-relating between those who are privileged and those who are most vulnerable.

———

How did this man, who prefers to be known simply as Peter, come to a place of understanding and commitment to such ideals? After participating in an MPT training, I set out to learn more about him and the work of nonviolence. Working with him on peace teams, and eventually becoming a trainer for MPT alongside him, I have had the privilege of listening to him as he tells the stories that shaped his life. When asked what drives him to do what he does, he said:

*The spirituality of nonviolence. We are supposed to keep growing until our last breath; there is awakening, self-actualization, understanding, wisdom, mysticism. Only a small percentage of the population reaches that state, but it is in the DNA of all human beings, this capacity for a higher mind. I want to be, as a human being, totally a lover of all people, of all nature, of all things. I am on the journey and urging everyone to be on the journey. It is possible in all of us. I talk on this, I work on it, and I strive for it.* [2]

Peter's journey began in 1934, born in Chicago but raised in Adrian, Michigan, with three older brothers and one younger sister. He attended Irish Catholic schools for twelve years, and along with playing basketball and football, he was the valedictorian of his class. His mother had been raised in wealth, as her father came from Czechoslovakia and founded a Bohemian beer company in Chicago. Peter's father grew up in Ontario, part of a poor family with his own father dying in a boxing match while trying to earn extra money for the family. Peter's father went into the Air Corps and trained to become a pilot, and he was eventually deemed acceptable in the moneyed family of Peter's mother. They married and lived a financially secure life until the Great Depression. They moved to Adrian, where his dad worked in a blue-collar job as a machine analyst until he died of colon cancer at the age of 63, just one year before Peter was ordained.

Peter recalls his mother as a good woman who did her best to deal with the dysfunctions of her family. Although usually known as a brilliant, funny, hardworking and respected man, his father was a drinker and every Friday night would come home from work drunk and violent and yelling. There was fear and terror in those times. As do most children who live in violent situations, Peter developed coping strategies and defense mechanisms to deal with the chaotic, fearful times in his childhood. He acknowledges that his motivation to become a priest was in response to this perceived powerlessness and internalized negativity. By being a priest, he would be someone important instead of a *"self-loathing insecure little kid."* With the help of one of his counseling professors, he did psychotherapy and came to understand how his exterior calm came from a deep fear of being criticized. He began to take off the mask he had made to cope with the challenges in his childhood and began to understand himself better. He realized that out of his own brokenness, he could find a way to empathize with other human beings. For him, this was the key.

Peter graduated from the parish high school in 1953 and went to the Detroit Sacred Heart Seminary for a bachelor's degree in philosophy, then on to four years of the seminary at St. John's Provincial Seminary in Plymouth, Michigan, receiving a bachelor's in theology. He was ordained a Catholic priest in 1961. His first assignment was in a working-class community in southwest Detroit, where he credits the people he served for truly teaching him how to be a priest. Many of the parishioners were Hispanic migrant workers, and he learned their language so as to better minister to their needs and understand their issues. The Cardinal Archbishop of Detroit then ordered him to go on for a master's in education from the University of Detroit, after which he served in Port Huron Catholic High School as guidance counselor and eventually as principal in 1966.

What he calls his transformation, or his conversion, began when he became the campus minister at Holy Trinity Chapel in Ypsilanti, Michigan, where he served the students of Eastern Michigan University. During this time, he finished another master's degree through the University of Detroit, this one in psychology with a certificate in psychotherapy and marriage counseling. His own psychotherapy was completing, and he felt a sense of contentment in his ability to help others heal and continue being healed himself.

It was the spring of 1970, when many students were rebelling and dealing with the war in Vietnam. At the time, Peter acknowledged, he hadn't really thought about war, rather following the ignorance of the era with an attitude espousing, *"I guess we have to fight and kill the communists."* But as young people came to him for counsel with concerns over the injustices of war and the destruction of life, property and relationships caused in its wake, Peter realized he had much to learn, and he needed to learn fast.

He started a macro analysis group of five, who read and studied issues about inequality, sexism, militarism, homophobia, classism, poverty and a host of other issues. They would get together after doing their readings and share what they had learned with the group. It was during this time Peter first learned and understood the effects of systemic violence, the effects of wealth and poverty, the role of empire in invading countries, overthrowing democratically elected presidents, and he soon started speaking out against the war himself. At the same time, Peter was exposed to and studied issues in the civil rights movement, the tactics and practitioners of Christian Nonviolence and what he felt was the call of Jesus of Nazareth to *"love your enemy and do good to those who hate you."* As his studies started to merge, he understood that *"the way to deal with the violence of the world was not to recycle violence but to seek and develop alternatives to violence."* [3]

From facing the violence in his family, to facing the violence of the Vietnam War, Peter sought further information on nonviolence. He read about people who espoused the strategies of Active Nonviolence — people such as Dorothy Day, Gandhi, Thomas Merton, Martin Luther King Jr., Liz McAlister, and Daniel Berrigan. He began to see the power of nonviolence and its effectiveness. For him, it was both a personal and social transformation, and he began to see nonviolence as a philosophy, a spirituality, a tactical strategy, and a way of life. He moved away from thinking holiness was tied to keeping the rules of the seminary and his religion. Rather, wholeness was about evolving in the stages of human development toward enlightenment and peace.

Striving for his own wholeness and self-transcendence, Peter was drawn to peace and justice issues. Always encouraging himself and others to work for the highest potential and for the greatest good, Peter notes:

*If you really want to change the world, you start with yourself. Start with your wits about you and continue growing. You're never done until you stop breathing. We can address the violence of the world and keep growing.* (4)

So, after demonstrating and speaking out in homilies during the five years he served at Holy Trinity Chapel in Ypsilanti, Peter decided he wanted to start living more congruently with the issues he considered most important. At the time, people active in liberation theology all over the world were taking risks and starting Abrahamic communities, as in Abraham of the Bible who led his people through the desert, never quite sure what was over the next hill. It was the summer of 1975 when Peter moved to East Lansing, Michigan, to form a Catholic Worker-type community, called the Abrahamic House. The house was a temporary shelter for up to ten homeless people at any one time. He used his time speaking for social change in various places in the community, particularly for the goal of nuclear disarmament. They relied on donated cars and donated food to support themselves, the "Abe House" and the homeless people they served. When available, he would say Mass at St. John's Student Center at Michigan State University, which is where I met him in the early 1980s. Peter admits he didn't have permission from the Church to join the Community, having not followed the expected process of going through the priest assignment committee. This didn't go over very well with the Auxiliary Bishop James Sullivan, who, at the time, called Peter into his office and told him he was a disobedient priest and a disappointment to the priesthood. Peter responded, *"I'm sorry you feel that way, Jim."* Nothing more was ever said, and Peter went on with his peace mission. About six months later, Bishop Kenneth Povish was appointed Bishop and he approved of Peter's ministry.

In 1976, Peter met Jasiu Milanowski, who had a Catholic Worker House in Grand Rapids, Michigan. Many communities and individuals across the state were banding together to work for nuclear disarmament, including those from Battle Creek, Detroit, Kalamazoo, and Lansing. As supports to each other, they held potlucks and gatherings to share and process their work for nonviolence issues. Realizing they were committed to much of the same work, Peter and Jasiu participated in the formation of the Great Lakes Life Community in the same vein as the already established Pacific Life Community, and the Atlantic Life Community. Groups such as these focused on nuclear disarmament and nonviolence, holding rallies, nonviolent protests, and acts of civil disobedience, which sometimes led to court and jail time.

Jasiu (pronounced "YA-shoe") was born to Polish immigrants and raised in Grand Rapids. At the time, it was a mostly conservative area of Michigan, with more churches per capita than anywhere else in the state. His family was friends with the family of Gerald R. Ford, the future president of the United States. When Jasiu was a young man, we worked as a page when Ford was a U.S. representative. He said that when he and Ford were on a stage and the crowd was angry, loudly protesting the war and the nuclear arms race, the chants were heated and tensions were elevating. This intensity unnerved Ford, and while seeing the look of vulnerability on his face, Jasiu also saw the power of people to impact their leaders with their voice and their numbers.

As a young adult in the 1960s, Jasiu started a printing business known as Print Kwik, and would often do printing jobs at cost for social justice groups. He became involved in the civil rights movement and was an original Freedom Rider, believing firmly in nonviolent actions for social change in America in order to bring equality and opportunity to the black community. He experienced trainings in nonviolence with the Southern Christian Leadership Conference in preparation to go into cities in the South to register people to vote. He worked alongside Dr. Martin Luther King Jr. on four occasions, and he met other iconic people from the civil rights era, such as Diane Nash and Jim Lawson. Those events and those encounters changed his life. The skills he learned at that time, coupled with a natural humility, brought the nonviolent battle for justice into focus as his life's work.

Jasiu was a student of life and an admirer of Dorothy Day and Peter Maurin, who founded the Catholic Worker movement in 1933. It was a movement founded on the principles of "personalizing" all people, caring for the poor, striving for a just wage, and empowering people of all stations to be valued contributors to society. Reading *The One-Man Revolution in America* by Ammon Hennacy so inspired Jasiu that when he began his own Catholic Worker House, he named it the Ammon Hennacy Catholic Worker House. In total, he had six homes in the Grand Rapids area under this name; creating a community that provided respite for the poor, promoted the skills of social justice, delivered food to those in need, and was grounded in the practice of Active Nonviolence.

Jasiu greatly admired the work of Gandhi, feeling inspired by this man who led a nonviolent movement for the independence of India. He read many books, studied his life and his beliefs, and emulated Gandhi's tactics of nonviolence to make change in his own country of America. Jasiu wrote a booklet called, "Gandhi: An Introduction." [5] In the booklet, he describes a term coined by Gandhi called "*Satyagraha*" (pronounced "sat-YAH-gra-ha"), which literally means "clinging to truth," but is often translated as "soul force" or "truth force." Jasiu wrote about Gandhi:

> *This force included nonviolent resistance and civil disobedience. He became convinced that 'Satyagraha' was clearly more powerful and effective than violent resistance and spiritually in tune with his values and ethics.* [6]

This idea became the central motivating force for Jasiu, the solid post on which to cling during tumultuous times. The idea of *Satyagraha*, which is the base of nonviolence, can and will be successful only if employed by what Michael N. Nagler identifies as "right means" in his book *The Nonviolent Handbook*. [7]

*We approach our situation with right intention. We are not and do not need to be against the well-being of any person. We employ right means. Wrong means such as violence can never, in the long run, bring about right ends.* [8]

This idea of "soul force" or "truth force" was the grounding philosophy for Jasiu throughout his entire life and drew him to work for peace through civil disobedience and nonviolence. Realizing the truth about war, he was "moved by the madness and the slaughter in Vietnam" and became a conscientious objector. Jasiu noted:

*There is a fundamental correlation between what you sow and reap; that is the point of the ends and means. It is pretty simple. You get what you do … I would tell people, 'If you rain bombs and death and destruction on people for a number of years, it's going to come back to you.' That is just the law of the universe, that ends and means are inseparable. So the means are everything.* [9]

Jasiu and Peter were part of the Great Lakes Life Community, which eventually evolved into the Michigan Faith and Resistance peace team. They mainly participated in actions protesting the nuclear arms buildup. In the late 1970s and 1980s, their focus for civil disobedience was at Williams International Corp. in Walled Lake, Michigan; KS Sawyer Air Force Base near Marquette, Michigan; and Wurtsmith Air Force Base near Oscoda and Lake Huron, Michigan. There were routine vigils, blocking of entrances, draping of banners facing the road in front of the plants, processions with pictures of people who had died in Hiroshima. Once, they went into the cafeteria of the military facility in Battle Creek and had a prayer service out loud. Signifying the blood being poured from the actions of our own country's military actions and the terrorism that resulted, they then poured their own blood on the floor of the cafeteria as the employees watched. Another time, the peace team lived for a week on the floor of a nearby gymnasium, and several members of the team would go each day to Williams International and block the entrance to the plant. Their last night, a plain clothes sheriff, who had been working under cover all week cooking food for the group, came to Peter and demanded he hand over all his papers and notebooks or they would search the entire group, totaling 30 people at the time. Peter told him he would not do this until he could meet with his group and come to a consensus decision on what to do. The sheriff patiently waited while the group discussed the implications of the decision. The team eventually came to a consensus that Peter would turn over his papers and notebooks, which he did. They confiscated his things and searched his body. They used this as incriminating evidence in trials for the people in this civil disobedience campaign over the next two years. Peter remarked of this:

*It is the irony of violence, that all these people working on non-violence have to go to trial and jail, but the people making the weapons and discharging them to kill people and communities don't. It is hypocrisy.* [10]

Jasiu, as well as Peter, spent their share of time in jail in various places, including Cook County Jail in Chicago; Marquette County Jail; Oakland County Jail, and Battle Creek County Jail in Michigan; Jacksonville (Florida) Jail; and Wisconsin Prison Camp. When Peter speaks of jail, his voice gets quiet and his eyes become distant. He notes a sense of dread, and his stomach turns.

He recalled the steel beds, and the benches and tables bolted to the floor. Typically he shared a cell with seven other men, sometimes more. Each of them would develop his own routine. Peter's routine was answering letters, praying, exercising, walking, talking with the guys, playing cards.

Once while in the Oakland County Jail in Detroit, Peter remembers when Don entered the cell. He was from the streets of Pontiac, about 50 years old. Don looked at Peter out of the corner of his eye and said in a low tone, "I'm gonna get you, Pop." Peter responded, "Don, you don't have to be afraid of me. I will never hurt you." Later that day, Don said it again, "I'm gonna get you, Pop." So Peter started worrying. A couple of the guys had heard Don, and went to Peter, telling him that if Don ever laid a hand on him, they would "beat the shit out of him." After that, Peter found himself worrying about Don. Peter tells the story like this:

*I came to a deep conviction, 'Don is my brother.' No matter what he does, I will not harm him. I will not hit him, I will not kick him in the groin, I will not smash his face against the cinder block wall, I will not do any of that. Don is my brother and I will not hurt him. I will do anything creative and I will protect myself, but I will not do violence. It was a powerful realization for myself. The next day, Don said it again. 'I'm gonna get you, Pop.' So I stood up and asked for attention. I said, 'This is an eight-man cell, life is hard in here. We have to work hard to get along in here. I wouldn't even want my dog living in here. So we have to get along and if one starts hurting someone else, the others would try to stop it.' I looked at Don and said, 'Don, you just threatened me again, and I've told you I will never hurt you. I want you to stop threatening me. Stop it.' At that instant, I felt a rush of power, I was taking back my power from the fear. I grew for myself in knowing Don and experiencing this. [11]*

Peter and Jasiu continued with the Michigan Faith and Resistance team and their efforts for nuclear disarmament and nonviolence. Thankfully, as the Cold War ended, many of the Strategic Air Bases and nuclear weapons production centers closed. The Michigan Faith and Resistance disbanded and people went their separate ways.

━━━━━━

The mission of nonviolence persisted in Peter Dougherty, Jasiu Milanowski, and many others who then worked together to start the Michigan Peace Team. Peter became the first coordinator in March of 1993. They formed a "core community" rather than a "board," as a team working together for consensus. Beside Peter and Jasiu, the core community also included Kay and Randy Bond, Mary Thomas, Georgeen D'Haillecourt, Wally Reese, and Jasiu's wife, Kerry Shaffer. Kerry often downplayed her role in the core, rather as the person who retrieved Jasiu from jail after his civil disobedience. But she brought many skills in conflict resolution to the work. As the core group worked together to determine their purpose and mission, it became apparent that if this group were to be a peace team serving domestically and internationally as it intended, it would need to provide training and educational workshops to do so. Each person brought his or her own experience and knowledge of peacemaking to the group. Peter brought his experience of working for nuclear disarmament, and Jasiu brought his experience of working with Dr. Martin Luther King Jr. and his training as a Freedom Rider during the civil rights movement. Together, they led their first Michigan Peace Team Nonviolence Skills Training in Flint, Michigan, in 1993 at the St. Francis Prayer Center.

Later that year, Peter and Jasiu went to Chicago at the invitation of Kathy Kelly, an internationally renowned peacemaker. Having been nominated three times for the Nobel Peace Prize, she was then working with an International Peace Campaign called "Mir Sada" or "Peace Now." The group needed trainers for their planned peace group to Bosnia and Jasiu and Peter were invited for that role. After the trainings, the International Peace Team went to Croatia, walked or bussed through the mountains to get to Sarajevo where the Peace Conference was held, calling to end the war. There were forty-four people from the U.S. who attended this Mir Sada in 1994, with five of those people from the Michigan Peace Team. Peter noted they learned a great deal about peace teams, and the multiple mistakes and mishaps that can occur with a large movement. It was an introduction to the work of peace teams and the potential to create nonviolent change. The learning curve had begun, and the Michigan Peace Team was on its journey to support Active Nonviolence.

Using their experiences with civil disobedience, Active Nonviolence, and the inspiring words of many who had gone before them, Jasiu and Peter and people of the MPT had committed their work to effecting change through nonviolence. Quotes stationed at various places at Jasiu's desk guided him in his life's work with the spirituality of nonviolence, reflecting a paradox of realism and hope. From Dr. Martin Luther King Jr.:

> For years, I've worked to reform our institutions, a little change here, a little change there. However, now I see we need something quite different; a reconstruction of our whole society and revolution of values.

Dorothy Day, the founder of the Catholic Worker movement and a visitor at the Ammon Hennacy Catholic Worker House Jasiu founded in Grand Rapids, had a statement that guided Jasiu in his daily life.

> None of us is in a position to change the world or transform the entire structure of our society; but we are all able to change certain things.

He admired Peter Maurin, an illiterate Frenchman who would stand on street corners to preach with humor on the societal issues of the time and the need for change. He worked with Dorothy Day in the establishment of the Catholic Worker House movement. He succinctly noted:

*The future will be different only if we make the present different.*

Each training and each peace team placed is an effort to allow change to happen in a nonviolent way. Peter and Jasiu have helped create a legacy with the development of the MPT. Over the years, the mission and vision of MPT have evolved. The mission is a guiding statement of what MPT wants to do, and the vision is how it sees the world as a result of its actions.

MPT MISSION: Building a just and sustainable world through Active Nonviolence.

MPT VISION: A just world grounded in nonviolence and respect for the sacred interconnectedness of all life.

With this mission and vision as the guide, there are Four Pillars of action for MPT:

1. Advocating for the power and efficacy of nonviolence
2. Training people in the skills of Active Nonviolence
3. Placing trained peace teams in places of conflict where invited
4. Networking and partnering with other peace and justice groups [12]

These pillars still support the structure and work of MPT, with a name change occurring in 2013. After celebrating its twentieth anniversary year, the name was changed to Meta Peace Team. The word "meta" implying the concept of "beyond" or "transformation." The work of MPT is beyond Michigan. It is beyond the typical answer for conflict, which is violence. It is transforming people and communities with examples of how nonviolence works and training people in the active skills and tactics involved in nonviolence.

There are peace teams deployed in domestic areas for a few hours or a few days, and into international areas for a few weeks to months. Always, there are rigorous trainings to prepare the team prior to being in an area of conflict, with the goal of de-escalating violence when tensions are high. Working with many other peace and justice organizations around the world, MPT aims to *"build a more peaceful planet through networking and collaboration."* [13] As the Meta Peace Team celebrated its twenty-fifth year in 2018, it was even more active with the challenges in income inequality, climate change, and human rights violations in our own country and abroad. Today, routinely there are calls for a Nonviolence Skills Training in communities across the country, and requests for peace teams at events where violence might erupt, given the divisive nature of our current political climate.

"Meta" is beyond the current paradigm of the fist, the club, the gun, the weapon, or the bomb as the answer to conflicts. Its aim is not to be rid of conflict, knowing this is impossible in our human family. But we can work toward a goal where people and countries can be in conflict without it degenerating into violence.

Inspired and motivated by other transformational leaders, Jasiu focused his interests and skills to make changes where he could in the area of nuclear disarmament using active nonviolent strategies. Coming from a family of violence and fear and feeling a sense of brokenness, Peter evolved and grew to understand the power of nonviolence, and he uses it as a tool to make societal change. Working together as Peaceful Warriors, Jasiu, Peter and the many people of the Meta Peace Team empower everyday people to choose non-violence as an active skill in dealing with conflict.

In the words of Peter Dougherty:

*We want to reach minds and hearts with our training and our actions. The Meta Peace Team is grounded in the spirituality of nonviolence, it is a philosophy, a way of life, with strategies and tactics that are tools of nonviolence. We are nurturing the interconnectedness of all people and all things. It is personal and it is social transformation. If we are not transforming ourselves, then we are recycling the violence.* [14]

*Rev. C. Peter Dougherty on a peace team*

## CHAPTER TWO

# WALKING THE TALK

*If you are dissatisfied with the way things are, then you have got to resolve to change them. —Barbara Jordan, civil rights leader and congresswoman from Texas, 1973-1979.*

Peter walks up my driveway, wearing khaki pants and a T-shirt that says, "Peace is Possible." He has come from the Michigan Capitol in Lansing, where he and a small group of people have been holding peace vigils every Friday since the Iraq War started. He carries his backpack and his thermos of black coffee everywhere he goes and enters my home with a sparkle in his eyes, ready for another interview session. The sun pours into the window onto the tiger oak kitchen table in my home as we take our seats with the tape recorder between us. From his backpack he takes his notes, his paper records in folders loosely bound, and hand-written outlines of the stories he wants to tell. He leans back in the chair and begins to talk.

*If we want to change the world, we need to start with our own transformation. The more we strive for this and work for it, the more the nonviolent strategies make sense and are easier. There was a time when I was paralyzed with people threatening me. As I grow and learn, I am more enlightened and able to let go of the fears, the powerlessness, the fear of being nothing, the fear of dying, the fear that I will resort to violence in my own rage. These fears can melt away as we grow deeper and become more and more aware. Can I be fully present? This is the purpose of my work, my meditation and my prayer.*[1]

As I listen to Peter tell his stories, I hear these themes come to life over and over with the people, the places, and all he has learned. What strikes me about Peter is his desire for growth and understanding, his continued efforts toward his own self- actualization, as well as his encouragement for others to reach their highest potential. He is consistent in this theme throughout our meetings. He role-models the journey for nonviolence with his continual efforts to educate people in the spiritual evolution that is possible for all of us. He has been walking this talk his whole adult life, and it doesn't matter if he has been 100 percent successful. The point is that he is consciously striving for wholeness and transcendence for himself and the world he impacts.

━━━━━━━

Working with Jasiu and the core community of the Meta Peace Team, Peter and the group routinely held eight-hour trainings throughout the area in 1994. The trainings were vital if peace teams were to be placed in areas of potential violent conflict. The first domestic peace team for MPT was placed in 1996 for the Keewenaw Bay Indian Community in Baraga, Michigan, on the L'anse Indian Reservation. Members of the tribe had a conflict with the tribal chair, Frank Dakota, and other council members, who had been personally benefiting from the financial deals they were making. When they removed 200 members of the tribe from their membership roll, essentially blocking those 200 people from receiving any of the financial benefits from the tribal casino, the offended members and their supporters took over the tribal headquarters in protest. Given the escalating tensions between the members and the tribal chief and his council, the members requested the presence of a peace team. For about six weeks a team of three peace team members, each working for two to three weeks at a time, acted as Unarmed Civilian Protection or Protective Accompaniment for the tribal members. At one point, the threat of violence was evident as the tribal chief said, "If it takes a body, it takes a body, but we are going to take back our headquarters."

Dakota sent in the tribal police, who used tear gas to disperse the crowd. It backfired, however, as the wind changed directions and the tear gas went back onto the police. The members reinforced the blocking of the entrance of the tribal headquarters and the peace team helped create a safe space for their occupation. Being careful to avoid taking sides, the peace team was present to create a safe space for each side. After about a six-week deployment of the peace team, Frank Dakota was charged with multiple felonies. He eventually went to prison for his actions.

Often, the Meta Peace Team would send members to be part of an International coalition peace team. Other organizations also send members including the Christian Peace Team and Pax Christi USA. One such coalition peace team was sent to Haiti in 1993. The country had long been ruled by the malevolent dictator known as Papa Doc. Born Francois Duvalier, he ruled with fear and death squads, collecting unofficial taxes from businesses and peasants. Upon his death in 1971, his son, Jean-Claude Duvalier assumed power and became known as Baby Doc. He continued the reign of terror with thousands of Haitians being killed or tortured by the death squads known as the Macoute. Peter recalls a story experienced by Liz Walters, a nun from the Immaculate Heart of Mary order, who represented MPT in coalition with Pax Christi USA and was stationed in Haiti. One morning while in a consensus meeting with the team planning the day's activities, they were suddenly interrupted by a frantic mother. *"They just took my son and they're going to kill him! Please help!"* The team immediately followed her to the home, where they found the Macoute death squad with a rope swung around the rafter of the house and looped around the neck of the terrified 18-year-old. Using the nonviolent tactic of direct intervention with the element of surprise and distraction, the peace team pushed past the death squad and removed the noose from the neck of the young man. They quickly escorted him out of the home and safely away, leaving the death squad behind feeling bewildered about the action. Their intervention saved the young man's life that day.

Baby Doc had been overthrown by a popular uprising in December of 1986, leaving behind a vacuum of power. He fled to France on a U.S. Air Force flight, while the U.S. Army placed temporary bases in the country to fill the vacuum. Many of the Haitian police sympathetic to Baby Doc fled into the hills afraid of the recourse of the Haitian people after years of abuse and terror, having been known as a brutal death squad with rampages across the country tying up the men and raping their women in front of them. It was during this tumultuous time that Peter served on a Christian Peace Team as a representative from MPT for this International peace team in 1994. He recalls hearing many stories of suffering, poverty, and violence, with one man saying, "I eat by accident."

A delegation of eight peace team members met with U.S. military leaders in Cape Haitian for over a week. There were attempts by the U.S. military to reinstate the police in the towns of Haiti, but the people of Haiti adamantly rebuffed this plan. People and their civil leaders gathered at town meetings to oppose the reinstatement, stating: "We never want to see these police again in our lives. Find us some electricity and water, not police." The peace team delegation met with Sergeant Stan Goff, in the town of Don Don, and Colonel Dubic in Cape Haitian. Concrete evidence of the previous police terror was requested and the concerns of the local people were gathered for the U.S. military with the support and presence of the peace team. The peace team worked with the U.S. military, discussing the nature of the situations in the villages and encouraged them to work with the civil society groups; meet with them, understand their chaos, become educated by the people in Haiti about the issues they faced. Peter gives credit to Goff who admitted the U.S. military was in as much a state of confusion as anyone in the country and was open to the support and suggestions of the peace team. They worked with the people in the communities rather than simply reinstating the abusive police. The presence of the peace team impacted the outcomes for those communities, as well as the perspective of the U.S. military.

The Meta Peace Team was also deployed to Chiapas, Mexico, starting in 1996. Indigenous Mayan groups were persecuted and harassed by the Mexican military and had declared war on the Mexican government demanding work, land, housing, food, health, and education. Despite their number, the indigenous people suffered extreme poverty, hunger and exclusion from governmental decision-making processes. They lacked basic human right services such as education and health care. Their plight was exacerbated by the passing of NAFTA, the North American Free Trade Agreement, which threatened the ability for indigenous farmers to make any living at all. Its own apartheid, the Mexican military often terrorized the indigenous people, keeping them from their farms, essentially starving them. International peace teams were called to be a presence with the Zapatista Communities. The Mayan groups had adopted their name from the historic and cultural icon, Emiliano Zapata Salazar, a revered independence revolutionary. They had planned a pilgrimage to the national capital, Mexico City, under the blessing and support of Bishop Ruiz, who stood with them. There would be danger from the paramilitary and military as they made their way from Cristobal through the state of Chiapas to the capital.

A team of eleven peace team members met with the bishop and were educated on the need for Protective Accompaniment. Wearing arm bands marking them as peacekeepers, the MPT members rode on buses through the major cities, including Oaxaca, allowing the Mayans to tell their story of oppression and voice their concerns for citizenship. In many cities they were met with support and processions to church services welcoming these indigenous people. There was no violence during their pilgrimage. Their Zapatista movement has been heralded as influencing many movements in the world including the Occupy Movement in America.

In the 1990s, MPT had a vision of placing an ongoing peace team in Tila, a northern region of Chiapas. Peter recalls that in a training for the Chiapas Mexico peace team, there was a man who drew concerns from the trainers. One of the role plays included a rebel coming into the home and forcibly taking one of the female team members. In the role play as a peace team member, this man lost his composure, becoming enraged at the rebels and started pushing and yelling. It was clear to all he was not suited for this type of peace team work. The role play was ended and a debriefing ensued about how some people are not the right fit for a peace team. Their skills can be used in other ways, such as fund raising, office work, marketing and networking. MPT trainings are a screening process to see if there is a mutual fit; the trainers screen the participants and the participants screen themselves and their abilities. Everyone has gifts and talents, and it is important to utilize and optimize them in the right place. As for the vision of the placement for an ongoing team in Tila, Kay and Randy Bond from MPT were a frequent peace team to the region. However, a more consistent presence was never developed because of financial constraints.

███████████

After pausing to reheat his coffee, I ask Peter to tell me a story of a time when he felt afraid as a peace team member. Figuring he would recall a particularly harrowing moment from one of the thirteen International peace teams on which he participated, I am surprised to hear him talk about the riots that erupted just outside the campus of Michigan State University after MSU lost a basketball game during the Final Four in 1999. MPT was called to the area, and as Peter and his team came down Bogue Street toward a large apartment complex, they saw people coming in from all over, not just students. More than 10,000 people were part of the riots, running through the streets, setting fires and vandalizing vehicles. Flames leapt into the sky as burning couches and furniture were thrown from second- and third-floor apartments to the ground below. Peter recalls "feeling fear in my gut." It was tough to walk toward the fire. The mayhem was already too far gone, and the time for peace teams well past as they looked at the mass of anger before them. Then they saw three young males rocking a car, trying to tip it over. Peter approached them, wearing his bright yellow Peace Team vest and said, "Do you guys really want to be doing that? This isn't you." The guys stopped what they were doing and walked away. Peter surmises his eye contact and calling upon their humanity in the face of mindless destruction is what stopped this particular incident.

Most college campuses have spirited game day activities, and Michigan State University is not unique in its tailgate celebrations on Football Saturdays. Given the history of the riot during the basketball season, the Meta Peace Team was called upon by the university to be present on campus for Football Saturdays, just in case there was any escalation of tension. One sunny Saturday, while tailgaters were getting ready for the game, a group of male college students were playing Frisbee on Munn Field. Amy Cairns and other members of her team were walking in the area when two men started arguing and their disagreement seemed to be heating up, with chests puffing, chins jutting to the air, and shoulders back.

Amy approached them and said, *"Hey, you guys are making me look bad. I'm supposed to be keeping the peace around here and you guys aren't helping me much."* [2] The guys stopped their posturing to look at her and her yellow Peace Team vest. They apologized to her and the team, and then resumed their game. Creative thinking on the spot defused tension and stopped a potential fist fight over a Frisbee game. Her interaction took less than a minute but may have made a difference for a lifetime.

Sometimes just being a presence is all that is necessary. The Meta Peace Team was called for such accompaniment for two young women who had recently graduated from Clinton High School in Clinton, Michigan. The two sisters and many from the school were challenging the community to rename their mascot, feeling the current mascot of "Redskins" was an inflammatory and derogatory racial slur and had outlived its acceptance as a high school mascot. Many in the town were threatened by this challenge and there were death threats sent to the young women. Their mother asked for the presence of the MPT at the scheduled school board meeting, where the young women would present their case. The peace team of three met them in the parking lot, accompanied the young women into the gymnasium, sat on the front row bleachers as they presented their power point, and escorted them safely back to their vehicle at the end of the presentation. Despite the overwhelming vote from the community to keep their mascot name, the young women were safe and successfully planted a seed for others to consider about labels and identity.

Much of the friction in our country and around the world is because of humanity's propensity for tribalism, or "other-ization." There is "us" and there is "them." Whether it is fear, domination, or insecurity, the separation of one tribe from another is fraught with tension. Part of this tension is the delicate balance between celebrating the unique attributes and culture of one tribe while also assimilating with the American tribe. Every year in Southfield, Michigan, an Arab American Festival is held. About ten to twelve city streets are blocked off for the celebration, which includes food, music, dancing, and artwork for sale. It is a festival in every sense of the word, attended not only by the Arab Americans in the area, but other faiths and various ethnicities as well. Most Arab Americans are Muslim, though some are Christian, some are agnostic and all are invited to the activities.

In 2010, there was a bit more tension brewing because of the public burning of the Quran by Reverend Terry Jones in Florida the year prior. A few days before the event, Jones announced he was coming to the festival. It was evident there would be supporters of Jones coming into the festival area, and threats of violence were mounting. The day before the festival opening, the mayor of Southfield contacted the Meta Peace Team and asked for help. Emails were sent to the MPT on-call list for an emergency peace team, and they were able to deploy forty people for the weekend event.

The event opened in the warmth of summer, drawing people from all over the region, as well as a gathering of supporters of Jones. Hate preachers, Christian fundamentalists, and nationalists spewed vitriolic words, calling out, "Muhammad was a pedophile," "Your mother is a whore," "You're going to hell," and "Are you saved?" In one area three fundamentalists yelled insults to rile a group of young men. Tensions were escalating and the peace team went to stand between the hate group and the Arab American youth. It soon became clear to the peace team that the perception was that the team was protecting the hate speakers, and this caused more tension. By quick consensus, the peace team decided to alternate which direction they faced; some toward the hate mongers, and some toward the festival goers, thereby communicating their efforts to keep everyone safe, not taking sides. This simple maneuver changed the dynamic and made clear the purpose of the peace team presence. It also de-escalated the tension in the area, essentially taking the wind out of everyone's sails.

Most of the festival was a joyous and celebratory event. Hours went by without any more incidents. Affinity teams — smaller groups of two to four members of the larger peace team — patrolled the areas, communicating with each other via walkie-talkie, keeping their eyes and ears open to the potential for conflict and the need for intervention. Affinity teams always stay together for their own safety purposes. While monitoring they noticed a group of about a dozen men, part of the fundamentalist nationalist extremists who had gathered in front of a store, were verbally taunting festival-goers. Peter and his affinity team were in the area, as were two or three police officers. The police and the peace team held each other in mutual respect, each appreciative of the other's presence and behavior. Suddenly, a young man reacted to the hate language and within seconds there was a melee.

The peace team immediately utilized the Third Party Nonviolent Intervention strategy of interposition. Peter and his team jumped into the mess and put their bodies between the fighting youth. The police did the same, without using their clubs or guns. Peter was hit in the face a couple times, with all the swinging arms and anger flying, but the peace team and the police were able to separate the fighters and calm the situation. The crowd dispersed and the only injuries were a few bruises and scratches. John, one of the MPT members, said, *"You can be on a peace team patrolling for hours and days, then in forty seconds all hell breaks loose, and you need to be there."* Like a life-guard at the pool, a peace team member must maintain constant vigilance and pay attention to detail. One cannot be lulled into complacency by the quiet. Peace teams must stay alert to subtle changes in energy, remaining present in the moment and ready to react as necessary.

Throughout the years Peter and Jasiu have been educators, leading countless training sessions. Sheri Wander, a core member of MPT, recalls her first time in the role as trainer. She was supposed to be an observer of Jasiu and Peter working together, but Peter was unable to attend at the last moment, so Sheri had to step into the role of co-trainer. She recalls that Jasiu gave her his complete trust and allowed her to find her own voice. She remembers seeing tears in his eyes when he would share a movie about the civil rights movement and the trainings with Diane Nash and Jim Lawson, because he had been there. She appreciated his ability to lead and let others utilize their skills in the work as well. It is more about learning the skills than taking credit for the work or the outcomes. Jasiu said:

> Whatever an education is, it should make you a unique individual, not a conformist. It should furnish you with an original spirit, a desire to take on challenges. It should allow you to find value that will guide you through life. It should make you spiritually rich, a person who loves whatever you are doing; wherever you are, whomever you are with. It should teach you what is important for you and the world, instruct you on how to fully live and the things worth dying for. [3]

Although some people in the peace movement seem larger than life, it has been the goal of MPT and its multiple trainers, including Jasiu and Peter, to empower everyday people to realize their ability to learn the skills of Active Listening, Nonviolent Communication and violence disruption. And to grow in the process. Most often, the skills are called upon to use in everyday life.

One day at the Catholic Worker House in Grand Rapids, a man boldly walked off with a sewing machine from the house. Jasiu, knowing Kerry often used the sewing machine for various projects, ran after the thief. When he caught up to the man, he said, *"Hey, we need that!"* and asked for the sewing machine to be returned to him. The thief put the sewing machine down and punched Jasiu, who fell to the ground. Jasiu got back up and retorted, *"Wait, what are you doing? That's our sewing machine!"* Again, the man punched Jasiu, and again he fell. Jasiu then told him, *"Man, why are you doing that? We just want our sewing machine back."* Finally, the thief said, *"Stop it, I can't do this to you anymore. Just take back the damn machine!"* Jasiu calmly rose and picked up the sewing machine and went home. He never responded with violence to the thief. Jasiu simply appealed to his humanity and asked why. The thief had no answer.

The nonviolent skills learned in a Meta Peace Team training give us tools for dealing with our daily lives as well as preparing people for the work of peace teams. Prior to any scheduled large peace team placement, there are multiple trainings held in the community to prepare for the event. This was the case in Indiana, when in 2001, a local peace group called upon the Meta Peace Team to be deployed during the scheduled execution of Timothy McVeigh. He had been sentenced to death by lethal injection for his role in the truck bombing at the Alfred P. Murrah Federal Building in Oklahoma City. That act of domestic terrorism killed 168 people and injured more than 600 others. Pro-death penalty factions and anti-death penalty protesters were expected in Terre Haute, Indiana, for the execution. Jasiu, Peter and other MPT trainers held a training workshop about a week before the event and invited people to be on the peace team the day of the execution. Many people from the area participated in the training and showed up as a peace team presence on the day of the execution.

Buses brought people in from all over the country. Authorities in Terre Haute had set up the area so that opposing protesters were separated from each other, with pro-death penalty supporters in one park and the anti-death penalty supporters in another park, miles away. People were then bused to their respective fenced area.

Peter was in the peace team that went to the anti-death penalty group. Some people were kneeling and praying, and at the time of his death, there was a solemn vigil. Suddenly, a loud preacher stepped up with a Bible in his outstretched hand and yelled, *"Are you saved? Do you believe?"* It was an alarming interruption to the silent vigil and Peter immediately went to him, engaging the preacher in a quiet discussion, while Jasiu interrupted an angry man who was starting to react to the preacher. Peter was still talking with the preacher when the execution was completed and people were being loaded back on the buses.

Among the people present was a man who had recently attended the MPT nonviolence training. He later told Peter he had been skeptical of the skills he had learned, but seeing de-escalation in action, he noted, *"This stuff really works."* He saw how Peter used what is known as the CLARA method with the preacher. CLARA refers to Calming/Centering, Listening, Affirming, Responding, and Adding Information. Peter was calm and listened to the man, then affirmed some of the similarities they shared. He also saw Jasiu calmly engage the angry man reacting to the preacher. He watched as this approach actually de-escalated the potentially volatile moment. These are the types of incidents that don't make the evening news, whereas if there were fisticuffs, it would have been plastered across our TV screens. This was the quiet, yet impactful work of the peace team.

Actions like this don't always come from a peace team, but could come from any individual who learns and practices these skills. An actual peace team is usually called for when there are numbers of people gathering and the potential for tension is high. As often as a peace team would be needed across our country, MPT goes only where it is invited. Given that political conventions tend to be a time for passionate displays of emotion and posturing on both sides of the aisle, MPT was invited to be a presence in Minneapolis, Minnesota, during the 2008 Republican Convention. There were multiple trainings held in Michigan and in Minnesota in preparation for the crowds outside the convention hall and more than eighty peace team members were present throughout the four-day event. MPT worked with local peace activists who also planned their own demonstrations and protests, but made it clear their purpose was to keep everyone safe, no matter what the identity group; Republican, Democrat, anarchist, non-anarchist, police, or non-police.

After a day of activities in the convention hall, people were leaving the event center. Protesters had been gathering all day outside the convention center and greeted the delegates as they were exiting. Police were present, trying to move people along and to disperse. Some protesters refused to leave. The police approached the peace team and asked for help in communicating to the protesters the need for them to move along and clear the area so parked cars could be moved and the congestion cleared. The MPT members approached the protesters and informed them of the situation and their need to clear the area, acting as a communication conduit for the police. The protesters peacefully complied with the request. All that was needed was effective listening and communication strategies for a peaceful outcome.

The next night, a rock concert was held in the Target Convention Center. The band was Rage Against the Machine, known for its incendiary politics and anthems of violent revolution. For weeks before the event, the media spoke of a potential clash. Police were concerned about the potential for tense interactions with protesters and concertgoers outside the Convention Center, and a large presence was ready with full riot gear, with mounted and bicycle police as well. MPT was also a presence as the concert ended. People mostly dispersed but about 100 concertgoers would not leave the area. Police used their bullhorns, *"Clear the area."* The concertgoers did not move. The peace team sensed the posturing and approached them, matter-of-factly stating that the police needed the street cleared, and that it was their choice to stay or to leave. However, if they stayed, there was a possibility the police would come through the area using their billy clubs. Then the peace team members went to the police and asked them to avoid the use of violence. In the end, the concertgoers moved along and there was no violence. Rather, the voice of reason and calm achieved the desired outcome. One bystander peace activist noted lives might have been saved that night with the actions of the peace team.

The presence of the Meta Peace Team was also requested at the 2016 Republican National Convention in Cleveland, Ohio. MPT partnered with other peace teams, such as Shanti Sena Network and D.C. Peace Team. The delegation patrolled the area offering a non-partisan, unarmed civilian peacekeeping presence, with the goal of creating a space for people to interact without violence, albeit in conflict. During one of the convention parades, a police officer on a bicycle moved along the yellow line on the street while protesters marched. He was riding close to the feet of a young African-American woman, and loudly instructing, *"Get to the right!"* The young woman responded and moved closer to the curb, but the bicycle policeman kept hitting her feet with his front tire. Having done as she was asked, moving as close to the curb as she could get, it was obvious the woman was becoming more anxious and irritated with the purposeful actions from the police officer. An MPT member witnessed this interaction and approached them, catching the eye of the police officer. Without speaking, the peace team member held out his hand to suggest this behavior stop, and the police officer rode off on his bike. The woman regained her composure and continued her march.

Later during the activities outside the convention hall, a white man slowly drove by, yelling and making obscene gestures to the protesters. A peace team member stopped and interposed herself between the protesters and the man in the car. With her yellow

Peace Team vest and her arms at her sides, palms open, the peace team member kept her eyes fixed on the man while the protesters passed behind her. The man grew silent and stopped gesturing, and eventually drove away. Nonviolence has its own power of intention and power of presence.

In July of 2005, Peter, as a representative of the work of nonviolence was invited to speak at the United Nation's Global Partnership for the Prevention of Armed Conflict Summit in Mexico City. The United Nations has convocations across the world on various issues and this gathering was focused on Unarmed Civilian Protection. He was one of a panel of four people, the others were all experts of the theory on nonviolence. Peter was the representative of on-the-ground experience. The other panelists were from Latin America. One in particular did not speak English, and, knowing some Spanish, Peter was asked to interpret. When it first came time for the interpretation, Peter giggles as he recalls he repeated what the person had said back in Spanish rather than actually translating into English. He stared at the people as they too laughed at his faux pas, then he clumsily did the interpretation. He admits he is much better at speaking the language than he is at interpreting. He spent four days in Mexico City for the convocation, which was attended by about 300 people from all over the world. He gave a Power Point presentation showing peace teams in action, working for human rights and creating a peaceful presence in areas of conflict.

———

Having settled in Holland, Michigan, Jasiu and Kerry became active in the Holland Peacemaker Group. There, they worked with the Baha'i community and their fireside chats, which addressed issues related to living within a community where conservative Christian practices and biases were prevalent. Some in the Christian community at the time had made attempts to keep other cultures out of the area. People from Cambodia, Vietnam, and Mexico were targeted. The Baha'i group, along with the support of Jasiu and Kerry, were trying to welcome these groups. They placed an ad in the local newspaper to start a group called the Alliance for Cultural and Ethnic Harmony, where people from different cultural communities were welcome to attend and share their belief system. They expected a handful to attend, but sixty people came to the first gathering. Wherever two or three are gathered, change is possible.

Jasiu and Kerry traveled often, having friends and adopted family all over the country from their various activities throughout their lives. While in Texas in 2015, Jasiu had a major stroke. He had been having mini-strokes for months but hadn't mentioned them to anyone. When the debilitating event occurred, he was brought back to Michigan and entered into Hospice care. Kerry recalls a constant flow of friends and family at his bedside. Staff would direct people to his room, saying, *"Go down the hall and turn left, then follow the noise."* There were children frolicking around, music was playing, stories were being told and there was much laughter. People came from all over the country to pay tribute. His obituary read:

> *As morning broke Sunday, September 13, 2015, Jasiu Milanowski (aged 69) breathed his last in Hospice of Holland at Medilodge, Holland, with Kerry Shaffer, his wife, constantly at his side and surrounded all week long with the love of many friends and family. At sunrise, Jasiu's great journey of peace and nonviolence ended. He was born July 23, 1946, to Wencel and Marguerite Milanowski. He attended St. Andrew Elementary School, Catholic Central High School (class of '64) and Aquinas College. He founded Ammon Hennacy Catholic Worker House in Grand Rapids. He was a co-founder of meals for the homeless on Bridge Street, at Capitol Lunch, and now God's Kitchen. In solidarity*

*with other conscientious objectors to the war in Vietnam, he worked as an orderly at St. Mary's Hospital. He was influential in founding the Calder Peace Protests, many peace groups in Grand Rapids, Holland, across the State of Michigan and beyond. He was a co-founder with Reverend C. Peter Dougherty of Michigan Faith and Resistance in the '80s, later to become the Michigan Peace Team in Lansing, and now the Meta Peace Team. He was also instrumental in founding the Alliance for Ethnic and Cultural Harmony in Holland, the Holland Peacemakers, and the Community Kitchen at Western Seminary. Jasiu was arrested and jailed for peaceful protests and nonviolent civil disobedience in opposition to war, nuclear weapons, and war taxes. He began and worked at Print Kwik. He loved skiing, and sailing his 36' Eastern Inner Club, named Satyagraha (after Gandhi's word for 'soul-force'). The Quaker Friends Meeting at Holland held a special place in his life. He loved music, especially jazz, bluegrass and folk. He read widely and lived faithfully the words of the Sermon on the Mount, Mahatma Gandhi, Martin Luther King, Jr., A.J. Muste, Walter Bergman, Franz Jaggerstatter, Gordon Zahn, Danilo Dolci, Lanza del Vasto, Dorothy Day, Eileen Egan, Daniel and Phillip Berrigan, Ammon Hennacy, Hildegarde Goss-Mayr, Jim Douglas, Farly Mowatt and many others. Jasiu was faithful to his calling as a disciple of peace and nonviolence. Peace was his clothing. Nonviolence his pen and his voice; mightier than the sword, gun, bomb, and war. Racial and social justice were his well-worn shoes. Compassion, his cap. Gentleness, his belt. Catholic Worker hospitality was in his hands. 'All we are saying, is give peace a chance' - his song. Love, his mission, message and the gospel in his heart.* [4]

Jasiu was greatly missed by the people of the Meta Peace Team, and Peter feels he lost a great friend. But in so many ways, his legacy lives on as the trainings and the peace teams continue.

Peter reflects on the work of creating peace, believing in his core that Peace and Justice are possible. He can see the slash and burn mentality in communities that are angry, or governments that are reactive and respond by dismantling laws for human rights. One of our interviews happened in a week where President Trump withdrew the United States from a long held Nuclear Arms Control treaty, Saudi Arabian leaders were involved in the murder of journalist Jamal Khashoggi without a firm response from the American administration, and eleven Jewish people were gunned down in their own synagogue by an anti-Semite white male nationalist. I asked Peter how he keeps going, how he finds hope in these difficult times. He quietly answered:

*Dorothy Day once said, 'We haven't got time to feel sorry for ourselves. There is much to be done.' This is one of those statements that keeps me going. The support of my community, of people doing this work, they keep me going. And being grounded in the spirituality of nonviolence; that this world is awesome and there is divinity beneath it all. The Divine is within it all, it is the animating force. And we are all part of that force.* (5)

As an answer to my own question, I am inspired by the words of Michael N. Nagler, founder of the Metta Center for Nonviolence in California, who said:

*Never be against people but only against problems. It is not me against you, but you and me against the problem; there is a way both of us can benefit and even grow.* (6)

Peter shares his favorite quote and it is one that appears on all his emails. It is the statement from Pierre Teilhard de Chardin; *"Love is the most formidable of all cosmic energies."* He thinks on this for a minute and looks up to say:

*There will have to be more massive nonviolent civil disobedience, massive non-cooperation. It needs to be a nonviolent revolution. But we need revolutionary patience. I may never see the fruits of what we do ... we have to be okay with that. All we can do is do what we are able to do, here and now. Don't complain about it, just do what you are able and do it together.* [7]

Sitting at my table, Peter has been so honest about the times he has felt unsure, times he has been pushed beyond his comfort zone, times he has taken risks to continue growing. He recalls his transformation from looking at the world simply through privileged eyes to understanding the systems of violence evident in racism, sexism, homophobia, xenophobia, war, and poverty. With each story, he reflectively states, *"This was an occasion to grow."*

I respond that he hasn't stopped growing yet. And he quickly adds:

*That's the point. To have the capacity to love and the courage to change life on Earth; this is desperately needed. We recycle too much of our own blindness. We are supposed to grow up, to have the courage to love and to change. We are still growing. I am grateful to those who have helped me grow and hope we can inspire one another to continue.* [8]

*Mary Hanna at the Meta Peace Team office*

CHAPTER THREE

# AN INOCULATION AGAINST VIOLENCE

*Never doubt that a small group of committed citizens can change the world. Indeed, it is the only thing that ever has. —Margaret Mead*

For some, their first exposure to nonviolence and the Meta Peace Team is seeing people wearing a yellow Peace Team vest. For others, like myself, their first exposure to the tactics of nonviolence and the Meta Peace Team is at a training. One of the pillars of the Meta Peace Team is: "Training people in the skills of Active Nonviolence." In order to fulfill this mission, Jasiu and Peter along with the members of MPT developed an eight-hour training. Along with the core skills of Active Listening, Effective Communication strategies, Bystander Intervention, and Third Party Nonviolent Interventions, the trainers include many opportunities for role-playing, using issues and examples that are pertinent to the group. Desiring to learn further nonviolent conflict management and communication skills, I had signed up for my own experience with the Active Nonviolence Skills Training in March 2017.

At the end of the Meta Peace Team training, we were asked to consider joining the MPT family and continue the work of nonviolence. I completed the form stating my interest in becoming a trainer and handed it to co-trainer, Katie Ames. As she accepted my form, she mentioned her plan to give it to Mary Hanna. I stopped in my tracks ... Mary Hanna? She was my roommate from college and I hadn't seen her for over 30 years! Sure enough, it was she. We got together and did the catch-up dance, sharing the many stories and experiences we had lived since our days on Spartan Street.

One can often hear her before they can see her. Mary Hanna, with her bursting belly laugh and distinctive voice is the glue that holds the Meta Peace Team office together. She sits at her desk, surrounded by tables with projects in various stages of completion. She spends her long hours keeping track of the who/where/when of the trainings, the peace teams placed and pending, and the general day-to-day workings of the organization. She first came to MPT in 2005, when her skills on the computer with data bases and management were needed. Starting as a volunteer updating the archaic system they had been using, Mary continued to increase her time in the office and eventually worked her way to a position considered "indispensable."

She started her career as a therapist with Community Mental Health in Lansing, Michigan. When changes in the system created a four-fold increase in her workload, she knew she couldn't provide the quality needed by her clientele, so she took an early retirement offered by the state for those with twenty years of service.

*I miss the clients, they were never the drain. It was the system and the endless paperwork. In a forty-hour work week, we were supposed to aim for eight hours of face-to-face time with clients, and the other thirty-two hours were for paperwork. It should be the other way around. It rewarded you for getting the paperwork done on time, but no value was placed on the therapy that was done. I just couldn't work in that kind of system anymore.* [1]

Beginning with the Meta Peace Team in technical support, she soon became the project manager and started working full time for MPT in 2006. Her path had crossed that of Peter Dougherty often in peace and justice activities across the state, starting in college when she would hear his homilies during Mass at St. John's Student Center while a student at Michigan State University. She recalls Peter would memorize the readings, then talk about them as if it was his story to tell. He would pair the reading with peace and justice issues of the day that illustrated the message in the reading, along with an urge to do something about it. She would see him at Michigan Faith and Resistance activities and at Williams International during protests over cruise missiles. According to Mary, *"He would sing songs of peace and consistently walked his talk. There is something really compelling about that."* [2]

The same can be said about Mary Hanna. Her commitment to nonviolence and the Meta Peace Team vision and mission is full. She notes, *"MPT is not just my job, it is my life."* [3] As well as her role in the office, she is a trainer, a team leader on deployed peace teams, and has participated in domestic and international peace teams throughout her tenure with the organization. She manages the social media for MPT, instructs the student interns on the workings of a non-profit, sells the Palestinian Olive Oil at various craft fairs to raise money for the organization, and stays late most days a week to make the many piles of work smaller.

Thankfully, she has some committed help in the office. Although listed as a part-time employee, Melody Arnst provides her expertise and knowledge in office management as if she were a full-time worker. Mark Zussman arranges the trainings and makes sure the calendar stays full. Mary Ashley volunteers and has become the go-to person to "git-'r-done." Before she retired in 2018 at the age of 84, Mary Ellen Jeffreys volunteered for many years in the same capacity. There are many people outside the office who commit every day to the goals and the work of peacemaking. None of the furniture matches, the desks are from various resale shops and the Lansing, Michigan office space is supported by Cristo Rey Catholic Church, the building in which it is located. Every penny raised goes toward the programs and trainings. Mary speaks fluently about the Meta Peace Team:

> *People feel like they are safe when the peace team is there; everyone, no matter what side they are on. This is a good thing. We don't squelch free speech, we are there to allow the sides to come together in a safe way, so they can figure out how to get along and interact. Our work is like a flu shot. Our work is an inoculation against violence. It isn't going to work for everyone, but it is going to work for many. We need to get more people inoculated.* [4]

As Mary talks about the skills and tactics of nonviolence, she often says, *"This stuff really works!"* The rational scientific mind in me then often wonders what proof she has for that confident statement other than anecdotal evidence, of which she has plenty. Some people believe nonviolence is naïve and weak. And, hearing of peace teams, they question the effectiveness of nonviolence tactics and doubt the ability to make lasting change that way. In response to such reactions, researchers Erica Chenoweth and Maria J. Stephan published their conclusions in the groundbreaking book, *Why Civil Resistance Works: The Strategic Logic of Nonviolent Conflict.* The team examined 323 cases of conflict from 1900 to 2006, evaluating major nonviolent and violent campaigns that were seeking regime change, the expulsion of an occupying force, or attempting secession.

> *This research is the first to catalogue, compare, and analyze all known cases of major armed and unarmed insurrections during this period. From this data, we find support for the perspective that nonviolent resistance has been strategically superior to violent resistance during the twentieth and twenty-first centuries ... Our findings point to a powerful relationship that scholars and policy makers should take seriously.* [5]

Chenoweth and Stephan found that nonviolent resistance campaigns were nearly twice as likely to succeed, compared to violent campaigns during the examined time period. About three out of four nonviolent campaigns succeeded, whereas one in four violent campaigns succeeded. [6]

Nonviolent civil resistance included boycotts, strikes, protests, sit-ins, stay-aways, and other acts of noncooperation and civil disobedience. The success of nonviolent campaigns was attributed to the active participation of a broader base of participants, including women, children, civil leaders, and people of all ages.

*Nonviolent campaigns have a participation advantage over violent insurgencies. The moral, physical, informational and commitment barriers to participation are much lower for nonviolent resistance than for violent insurgency. Higher levels of participation contribute to a number of mechanisms necessary for success, including enhanced resilience, higher probabilities of tactical innovation, expanded civic disruption, and loyalty shifts involving the opponent's supporter.* [7]

In other words, there are barriers to participating in violent campaigns, including loss of life, income, home and community. Often, there are moral disagreement with the means. These barriers are not as prevalent in nonviolent campaigns, which can therefore attract a wider base of participation. It was also found that nonviolent movements resulted in longer lasting peaceful change. Chenoweth and Stephan note:

*The transitions that occur in the wake of successful nonviolent resistance movements create much more durable and internally peaceful democracies than transitions provoked by violent insurgencies. On the whole, nonviolent resistances are more effective in getting results, and, once they have succeeded, more likely to establish democratic regimes with a lower probability of a relapse into civil war.* [8]

When evaluating the violent campaigns:

*Our statistical evidence suggests that countries in which violent insurgencies exist are more likely to backslide into authoritarianism or civil war than countries when nonviolent campaigns exist, which often become more stable democratic regimes.* [9]

These quotes and this research aren't just fabrication and opinion-mongering. It is real data that is retrospectively evaluated and compiled to compare the effectiveness of violent insurgencies and nonviolent campaigns. The data strongly support the creativity, courage and effectiveness of civil resistance. From the black and white students sitting at the lunch counters in the 1960s working for civil rights, to the People Power Movement in the Philippines, which forced dictator Ferdinand Marcos from power after violent challengers failed to do so in the 1980s, nonviolent movements work, and they have lasting effects. The cost of violence is greater — financially and in lives and communities lost. Nonviolent movements may, however, take more time, more courage, more patience and more collaborative effort to bring multiple disparate groups together for a common goal. It may not be as glitzy for the evening news as waving a banner saying "Mission Accomplished" or carrying out a bombing action called "Shock and Awe," but the conclusions from Chenoweth and Stephan could make a real and lasting difference in policy making, leadership in our country and on a global scale. If we let it.

Nonviolence not only works, but research has revealed that it is the best tactic and strategy for lasting change to break the cycle of violence. Mary often says, *"If the only tool in your tool box is a hammer, then everything looks like a nail. Our job is to look for more tools."* [10]

The Meta Peace Team and the trainings teach us about the many possible tools in the tool box. Being on a peace team gives us the opportunity to use them. But in our daily life with family, co-workers, friends, and with strangers we meet everywhere, there are opportunities to use these tools.

———————

It was one of those spitty wet snow days in March 2018 when Mary and I went to Kalamazoo, Michigan, to conduct a Bystander Intervention training for the Church Women United annual gathering. Mary drove and we spent the ninety-minute trip going over the itinerary, brainstorming on what role plays to use and assigning the various parts of the training between us. Each training is slightly different, taking into consideration the audience and the issues important and possible for them. We try to make the examples and the role plays applicable to the participants and their reasons for being there. As we traveled along I-94, we developed a solid and workable plan. It is typically a four-hour training, but we had two hours for a training on Friday afternoon and again on Saturday morning. We arrived with time to spare and set up our equipment for the event. Then we waited.

It turned out that the timing of the various speakers for the event were not kept to a strict schedule and things were running behind. So we quickly adjusted our plans. Mary told me that the value of flexibility and the ability to adapt to swiftly changing circumstances is a great skill to have on a peace team. Eventually it was our turn to present. We did the best we could on Friday, but Saturday morning we had the entire allotted time to do the short version of Bystander Intervention training.

We started with a Centering Exercise and for this part, I read the words of the song, "*Make Me a Channel of Your Peace.*" We introduced ourselves and the work of the Meta Peace Team, then instructed them on the concept of Bystander Intervention. Mary told a story of her own, to illustrate the actions and how each of us can do this work every day. She was walking to her car in a parking garage after work one day, and overhead a mother yelling at her child while standing outside the car door and hitting him with a shoe. Mary slowly approached the woman and said in a calm voice, *"Are you okay, you seem really upset. Is there something I can do?"* The mother stopped what she was doing and looked at Mary somewhat exasperated, then slightly embarrassed. *"No,"* she replied, looking down at the ground. *"He just won't put on his shoes. You know how kids are."* Mary then commented on how it had been a long day, and how tiring that can be. She then looked at the child, and asked, *"Are you okay?"* Once he sheepishly nodded, Mary touched the mother gently on the arm and said, *"It can be really hard and sometimes it's all we can do to take a deep breath and walk away."* She wished them a better day and proceeded to her car, hoping that by aligning with the stresses of the mother rather than shaming her behavior, the interaction would leave the mother with something else to consider. The woman got into her car and they, too, left the parking garage.

With this example we talked about the elements of Bystander Intervention, how simply distracting or interrupting the behavior can either stop or thwart the violence. It may take only a few minutes, but it can make a difference in the long run. We'll never know what happened to the mother and her child after this incident; if she was contrite and sorry, or if there was a more severe beating once they were home. But for that moment, there was a pause in the injury and the child witnessed a bystander attempting to change his situation. They were not alone.

It helps to hear actual stories that illustrate the skills of Bystander Intervention. For instance, a white woman tells a story of standing in line at her local grocery store, watching the cashier as she gets payment from the black woman ahead of her in line. The cashier seems to be taking a great deal of time, checking the "bad check" list, and asking for multiple pieces of ID. She knows the customer ahead of her as she has seen her there before and other places around town. Although the white woman is somewhat new to the area, she has never been treated this way at the checkout. She waited until the cashier was done, then approached with her groceries. She asked the cashier why the woman ahead of her was treated differently from herself. *"Well,"* stammered the cashier, *"she is new to the area. And it's our policy."* The white woman politely pointed out that she herself was newer to the area, and had never been asked for multiple pieces of ID. Upon exiting the grocery store, the white woman caught up with the customer who was ahead of her in line, and let her know she had witnessed the event and found it unacceptable. She intended to inform the manager of the store of the behavior, which she later did, and wanted to share that information with her.

This is an example of delaying our actions until a more appropriate time to intervene. It would not have been helpful or appropriate to intervene during the transaction with the cashier, but it would be appropriate to point out the discriminatory behavior and follow up with the manager of the store. Letting the other customer know what she saw may help that customer not feel so alone.

A Bystander Intervention role play for a high school group could be the opportunity to intervene when a classmate is being bullied. The setting is a high school classroom as students enter for the period. As one of your classmates walks in, you hear someone in the "jock" group make a snide remark about the degree of acne on his face and the challenge it will pose in getting a date to homecoming. What can you do?

With a *Direct Intervention*, you could approach the bully and call him out for saying such a hurtful thing. This may not go over so well, as now you could become the focus of his attacks. However, saying *"shut your trap"* may bring you some satisfaction and send a message. Unfortunately, one's position in the pecking order in high school often dictates the potential realistic response.

With a *Distracting Intervention*, you could start singing *"Happy Birthday"* to the person who was bullied after the hurtful statement. For one, it might embarrass the bully who just made fun of someone on their "birthday," and two, it could diffuse a potentially painful situation for the bullied.

The use of the *Delegation Intervention* seeks the help of others in the situation. Informing the teacher of the actions of the bully may help the adult leaders in the school address the situation in the future.

The use of the *Delay Intervention* entails speaking with the bullied student later after the incident and letting them know the behavior of the bully was rude, reflecting more about the bully's poor self-esteem and need for attention, than about the bullied student.

While engaging in Bystander Intervention, it is important to first ask if there is anything we can do to help. There are times when if we just jump in and "rescue" someone, we take away their control or their agency and can potentially make things worse. It is a gentle art to consider, as sometimes, when there is abusive language or potentially escalating interactions taking place, we need to use distraction, direct action to intervene, or delaying our response until the situation is safer. There is no ONE right way to make a difference.

On our way home from the Bystander Intervention training, Mary told me a story of participating on a peace team at the Gay Pride Event at the Capitol in Lansing. Typically, people march down Michigan Avenue, waving their flags and celebrating with friends and loved ones. There are commitment ceremonies held on the Capitol steps, then people make their way to the festival grounds at the river for more fun and festivities. Every year, evangelical ministers gather at a corner on the parade route, where they hold signs and shout statements like *"You're going to hell!"* and *"God hates fags!"* One year, a group of rather inebriated young men who were participating in the march came upon the yelling ministers, and the young men started singing at the top of their lungs, *"Jesus loves me this I know!"* The ministers retorted, *"Jesus hates you! You have no right to sing that song!"* As it started to get intense, an MPT peace team member ducked under one of the outstretched arms of a minister and into their group, yelling, *"Singing? Did I hear we're gonna sing?"* And she started singing loudly *"If you're happy and you know it, clap your hands!"* You simply have to clap your hands when you hear that song. So everyone on the parade route joined in and they moved along down the street past the flabbergasted ministers. The bystander art of distraction saved the day and decreased the rising tension on the corner.

The Gay Pride Event is held every year in June, and the Meta Peace Team has fielded a peace team for many years. At first, the police told them to *"stay out of our way,"* communicating concern that the peace team would be a distraction and eventually need the help of the police. The peace team would remind them they were simply there to protect people from violence, no matter what the source. Year after year, they would see the peace team's presence at the Pride event. Eventually, the police would recognize the value of having MPT present, and give a respectful nod in the direction of the peace team members. There became a mutual respect for the role each played during the event.

One year, the marchers included a man whose son had recently died of AIDS. It was his first time marching in the event, and it was obvious he was distraught. He was heartbroken and marching in tribute to his son. As he passed the evangelical ministers, there was a preacher who yelled at him, *"Your son didn't know anything about love, he's burning in hell right now!"* This enraged the father who then started yelling back and getting into the minister's face. A young police officer started toward the altercation while reaching for his baton, but the police chief placed a hand on the officer's arm and said, *"Stop. The peace team will handle it."*

And they did. One peace team member went up to the father and engaged him in conversation, *"I'm so sorry to hear about your son, please tell me a little bit about him."* And they gently led him away from the ranting ministers. Another peace team member engaged the minister saying, *"I don't know much about scripture, but am really interested in where it speaks of this, can you tell me more about it?"* The tense interchange, which could have resulted in blows, was de-escalated with the nonviolent tactics of distraction and inter-positioning. Much like disciplining small children, it is an interruption of the behavior, redirecting the participants to something else, and then reinforcing new behavior. There was no need for a weapon, or a baton, or any level of violence.

Mary has been on many peace teams and usually carries the walkie-talkie, staying in contact with the other affinity teams that have dispersed throughout the area. At a so-called "Right to Work for Less" rally held in response to anti-union legislation signed by then Michigan Governor Rick Snyder, the Meta Peace Team was invited to be a presence. It was a very cold January day, with temperatures in the 20s. Despite the conditions, there was a formidable crowd at the steps of the Capitol in Lansing to protest the legislation. Off to the side was a tent purchased and placed by a wealthy Michigan business family, as a counter protest at the rally. A representative of the wealthy business family was yelling and essentially telling the union supporters how naïve and stupid they were for joining a union. This message didn't go over well with one particular woman, who started a back-and-forth interchange that became heated despite the frosty air.

When it became apparent that someone might get punched in the mouth, Mary's affinity team went to work. She placed her body between the two arguers and, with her back to the man, Mary engaged the woman in a discussion.

*Excuse me, my name is Mary. I don't mean to interrupt your conversation, but I was just wondering, does your thermos really work?" The woman just looked at Mary surprised, so Mary continued, "I am always getting thermoses and they just don't keep my coffee warm. Where did you get it? How much was it? Do you think they still have any?*

The woman kept having to field Mary's multiple questions, and in the meantime, other members of her affinity team had approached the man and politely told him he should come with them. Given the rising tensions in the crowd, it was in his best interest to leave the area. MPT used Protective Accompaniment to escort the man away from the area to safety.

After a while, the woman finally responded, *"Just take the damn thermos. And I wasn't going to hit him anyway."* She had figured out what was going on, and it gave her time to calm down.

Mary reflected on the incident.

*It doesn't have to be about convincing anyone. It is about allowing enough time to let someone regroup, rethink, and get ahold of themselves before they do something they could regret or even hurt someone. MPT allows people to connect with the part of them that knows. We buy people time to make a different decision.* [11]

At another rally at the Capitol, this one for Women for Gun Sense, Mary was again part of the MPT peace team. Milling through the crowd, the affinity teams kept an eye out for anything suspicious or potentially violent. Hours can sometimes go by without an incident at rallies such as this. But on this sunny day, a man was standing on the edge of the crowd wearing a full bandolero across his chest with an arm on his semiautomatic rifle. The affinity team kept an eye on him as they made a plan and communicated the plan via walkie-talkie to the other peace team members and their affinity teams spread around the grounds. Wearing her bright yellow vest, Mary made her way through the crowd and then quietly stood near the man. She edged her way closer to him.

*"Wow, what a pretty day!"* she said to him.

Secretly, she was wondering what would prompt a man to come to a "gun sense" rally carrying a gun like this, but she had an insight. *"I was also thinking that this guy is really afraid. I wondered how I could help make him feel less afraid."*

Eventually the man replied: *"Peace Team, huh? What do you think you're gonna do?"* Mary answered, *"We are just here to make sure everybody stays safe."* The man responded, *"Well, if anybody bothers me, I have my gun,"* and he patted the weapon strapped across his chest. Mary thought about it for a second and said, *"And I am just here to make sure you don't have to use it."* (12)

She saw her message sink in, his face reflecting surprise, as it never occurred to him he would be protected by anyone with something other than a gun.

> *Nothing big happened, because we do these little things. Sometimes even just looking at someone and seeing them, meeting their gaze. It helps them calm down, or it diffuses the situation. Wearing these big yellow vests that say 'Peace Team' changes the dynamics and the energy just by reading the word 'Peace.' We don't get direct feedback, we don't know what we've thwarted, what seeds we've sown for the future. This has to be enough.* (13)

I served on my first peace team with Mary on March 5, 2018. In Michigan, the weather in March can be either winter or spring, and sometimes both in one day. This day, it was cold and gray, but there was no snow or rain in the forecast. After much deliberation, Richard Spencer, the so-called white supremacist, was going to be speaking on the campus of Michigan State University. He was allowed a limited time in a designated area. Given that it was spring break, there weren't many students who stayed around for this event. The location was on the southern-most aspect of the campus at the large animal pavilion where rodeos and auctions occur, away from the hub and bustle of the university. Area peace groups, religious organizations, health and education providers had organized a counter protest at All Saints Episcopal Church just off campus to the north. It was to be a Peace Festival; with face painting, decorating rocks with positive messages to place around town, great food, and a slate of musicians to play for the evening. The Peace Festival organizers of the event asked the Meta Peace Team to be present at their event. Despite multiple attempts to place a peace team at the corner of Bogue Street and Mount Hope, adjacent to the pavilion, MPT was not invited. Instead, more than 300 police officers from around the area were deployed in anticipation of violence.

Eight other members of the peace team and I met for an hour prior to the festival. We were briefed on the activities of the event; speakers outside, food inside, followed by music and family activities. There would be two affinity teams, and there was a leader in each team with a walkie-talkie. We donned vests and walked through the hallway and the gathering crowd. As we walked through the crowd, there were cheers and clapping and big thank you's being said by many. It was almost an atmosphere of joviality, not a potential for harm in any way. But we knew to keep our eyes open and remain vigilant.

Throughout the evening, the peace team members patrolled the area in and around the church, keeping eyes and ears open for anything suspicious. A patrol car was stationed at the entrance of the parking lot with two police officers assigned to the festival, and we kept in communication with them about the events occurring at the pavilion. Only about fifty people attended the presentation by Richard Spencer, but about a hundred protesters came in from all around the country. There were a few minor skirmishes at the corner, punches thrown and taken. It would have been an ideal place for a peace team presence to de-escalate this violence, had we been invited.

As the last Peace Festival speaker finished his message, most people moved inside the church for food and music. A disc jockey piped music into the parking lot and the peace team patrolled the area as hundreds of people from the community came and went. It was a party-like atmosphere, and even members of the peace team danced in the parking lot to stay warm as the chill of the day started to settle. With only forty minutes left of the event, a truck pulled up and a white man in a winter coat got out and walked into the parking lot while the truck drove away. Mary immediately informed the other affinity team to keep an eye on him. From our different positions, we all kept our gaze on him and stayed in communication with each other. He walked through the parking lot and was greeted by two of our peace team members, as we had greeted everyone who came that day. He walked around the building to the opposite door and tried to get in, but the door was locked. So he came back to the parking lot and went into the main entrance. Mary and I followed.

Inside the hallway, it was crowded and warm with people. Someone stopped us to take a picture, and although I was slightly distracted by this request and thought about stopping for a photo. Mary was all business and kept her eye on the man while she politely told the photographer we *"were working."* The man walked to the end of the hallway, and turned left into the area where a meeting room for quieter conversation had been set up for the festival. Mary followed. Seeing that there wasn't much going on in this hallway, he turned around, and ran right into Mary. She distractedly asked him where the meditation room was located, and he said he didn't know. He then re-entered the main hallway leading to the community hall where most people were gathered. People were sitting and standing all around the large room, eating and listening to the musicians in a coffee-house style arrangement. By now, the entire peace team, the minister of the church and the two policemen knew of his presence and were on guard.

I entered the large community hall and stood with my affinity partner, Terry Link, off to the left by the wall. The musicians were on the right, and all through the hall people were sitting and standing listening to the music. The man had entered the room and stood at the far end off to the left. Two other affinity teams took their position by the back door on the right and at the entrance. We kept our eyes open and acted like we were listening to the music.

Sitting at a table near me was a young woman with a hijab head scarf. She stood up and I noticed there was open space between the man who was now standing some distance off to my left and this woman. I quickly placed my body between them, with my back toward the man and faced the woman, making small talk about how lovely her sweater looked with her scarf. I didn't think about my own safety, or if he even had a gun hidden in his coat, but I thought it important to be a buffer between them. Our conversation ended and she left the event unaware of the potential risk.

The Peace Festival activities ended and people started leaving. The man we were tracking made his move to leave, and we monitored him as he again tried to leave from a different door. He was eventually guided by the minister to leave from the door he had entered. He told her he had been to the other speech and just wanted to see what was going on at this event. She thanked him for coming. Some of the peace team members were escorting people to the parking lots, while some of us watched as he walked a couple blocks away to the waiting truck who then picked him up and they drove away.

After the festival-goers had cleared, the members of the peace team met for a debriefing. We discussed what went well and what could have been improved. We shared our experiences of the evening. I was grateful for the guidance and example provided by the more seasoned peace team members, Mary Hanna and Katie Ames, the two leaders for the event. I felt like it was a pretty fun time for a while, dancing in the parking lot to stay warm, but then the acute sense of vigilance and monitoring was put into play. I was glad the minister had engaged him in a bit of a conversation, so he didn't feel stalked. Although there was nothing violent and the risk was low, there was a real lesson in the work of a peace team. I was glad to be a part of it as witness and as participant.

When Mary talks about MPT, there is conviction in her voice when she speaks of the effectiveness of nonviolence. It is using a bigger tool box with many more tools than a hammer. It is making a difference in people's lives by inoculating them against the ravages of violence by giving people other ways to approach conflict. It is listening and affirming our shared humanity. Mary notes:

*I have a much better chance of making a positive difference if I deal with people with care and compassion rather than with anger and hate and violence. No one remembers a positive impact on their life from someone treating them like shit. We remember that positive impact when we are treated with respect and compassion and gratitude.* [14]

*Kim Redigan (right) on a peace team*

## CHAPTER FOUR

# SPACE MAKER FOR PEACE

*Be patient toward all that is unsolved in your heart*
*And try to love the questions themselves.*
*Do not seek the answers that cannot be given you*
*Because you would not be able to live them*
*And the point is to live everything.*
*Live the questions now.*
*Perhaps you will gradually without noticing it*
*Live along some distant day into the answers.*
*—Rainer Marie Rilke*

If you need something done, ask a busy person to do it. Whoever first noted this may have been referring to Kim Redigan; who is a full-time high school teacher, a trainer for the Meta Peace Team, routinely works for peace and justice issues with Pax Christi Michigan, People's Water Board Coalition, Michigan Coalition for Human Rights, and frequently participates in peace teams both domestically and internationally. I had a hearty breakfast ready for her during an interview she was able to schedule prior to the Core Meeting for the Meta Peace Team on a Sunday morning.

She would say that from the time she was a little girl, *"there was a fire in my bones for justice."* [1] Kim was born into a blue collar, working-class community in Taylor, Michigan, which is down river from Detroit. As she entered kindergarten, U.S. Marines were entering Vietnam, and Saigon fell the year she graduated from high school. All of her formative years were framed by the issues and events of the Vietnam War. Many of the boys in her neighborhood went to Vietnam and many of them did not come home. Christmas was usually difficult for Kim to enjoy, knowing that people in Vietnam were being burned, maimed or dying in the war. She couldn't bear the injustices she saw on the nightly news and heard discussed in all corners of her neighborhood. Kim would write poetry or stories, trying to find an outlet for her angst. Given her idealistic and sensitive nature, but without role models or guidance in how to channel this in a healthy way, Kim struggled with depression and used alcohol to cope.

Alcohol became the way to block out the sadness, the fears, the realities of violence and dysfunctions of war. Despite the overuse of alcohol, she made her way through an undergraduate degree in college with what she calls the *"A or W plan; I either got an A in the class or I withdrew from it."* [2] Realizing there was another way, Kim entered a 12-step program, and she worked to became sober. Feeling called to Catholic Social Teachings and the writings of Dorothy Day with her Catholic Worker movement, Kim became involved with issues of peace and justice, poverty, equality, and human rights. She stayed active in her program and became a sponsor for others while focusing her drive for justice with anti-apartheid work, activism in El Salvador and working to become certified as a teacher. She had married her partner, Matt, and together they had four children. As she held her babies she realized a deep conviction that war made no sense, and that being a mother meant caring for all children, not just her own. Whether born in Iraq, Palestine, South America, El Salvador, Chicago or anywhere, all children deserved to be safe from harm. It was in the year 2000 when her parish, St. Thomas Aquinas on the west side of Detroit, held a Meta Peace Team training taught by Peter Dougherty and Mike

McCurdy, who had just returned from a peace team trip to Palestine. Kim attended and felt like she had found a spiritual home.

Kim took to MPT like a fish to water. It was August 2001 when she realized deep in her gut that her life would be changing in ways she was not yet aware. Then September 11th happened, and Kim felt her activism and nonviolence skills converging — peace team work was the work she felt born to do.

By then, Kim was teaching high school. Not only does she teach in the areas of English and theology, but she incorporates justice and civil rights issues into the curriculum as well. She takes groups of students on immersion trips to El Salvador, to civil rights tours in the South, and is a role model with her peace and justice work. Kim has transformed her own history of depression and alcohol abuse into an understanding of the human condition. She consciously balances her outer work with the inner work she does on a daily basis.

*Having been through what I have gone through, brokenness doesn't scare me. Mental illness doesn't scare me since I have mental illness in my family. When we go into places, standing before even the most vile hate mongers, something comes over me on a peace team like a cloak from God; profound compassion. You see their brokenness, even in some of our leaders. I look at them and can feel very angry and know they need to be stopped, but there is also a deep compassion that there is something very broken in them to cause them to act the way they do. Fear and love are the driving forces in our world. The Meta Peace Team asks us to meet fear with a spirit of love. It changes the energy.* (3)

Kim embraces the 12-step program, feeling her whole spirituality is forged with these tenets. If we come from a place of fear, where we feel shamed and vulnerable without agency or control, we have a recipe for violence. But as a peacemaker, we can recognize our existential powerlessness in the world, realizing we only have this very moment.

*I wish everyone had the opportunity to recognize our powerlessness, and our dependence on something outside ourselves, even if it is our community. The world would be a different place if we could all have a willingness to take our own inventory, starting with ourselves first and making amends where they need to be made. Then we can have our own spiritual practice as we identify ways to serve others. This is my spirituality.* [4]

Her work with the Meta Peace Team is what she calls her spiritual base. She describes this work as active, bold, creative, and nonviolent. [5] The work is active, she says, in that we are actively using tactics to create space for people to interact and address their differences; bold in that it takes courage and audacity to be present in this work; creative because we need to think on our feet, color outside the lines and try new things; nonviolent because violence never solves anything, it just postpones solutions.

A photograph on the wall in her classroom illustrates this active, bold, creative, nonviolent work. It was the Arab American Festival, on a hot summer day in Dearborn, Michigan. The Meta Peace Team was asked to place a peace team in the area because extreme Christian fundamentalists were coming to town. Their ideology was similar to opinions of Terry Jones, who had preached to burn the Quran. The fundamentalists held signs touting *"Muhammad is a pig"* and *"Islam is going to hell."* It went beyond Islam as they slammed Catholics, Jews, gays, and blacks, too. Their point is to provoke someone to cross the line and react in anger, and when they are the recipient of an angry violent outburst they become the "victim," often suing for damages.

On this particular day of the festival, their target was a young woman in her mid-teens, wearing a hijab. She was there with her friends, and the women on the peace team were trying to be a presence by providing a buffer between them and the yelling fundamentalists. The peace team encouraged the woman with the hijab and her friends to ignore the taunts. *"Your mother is a Muslim whore, you're a whore and you're going to hell!"*

Then the fundamentalists started yelling at the women on the peace team. *"Look at you women wearing trousers, you're all whores and sinners. You should be home cooking for your husbands."*

The members of the peace team worked with the young women who had been targeted by the fundamentalists, and together they started using hand motions as they loudly sang, *"Stop! In the Name of Love,"* a song made popular by Diana Ross and the Supremes. They tried to make it fun while doing their best to ignore the repetitive taunts of the hate mongers.

Kim describes what happened next:

*Then this young woman, on her own without prompting, went across the street to the dollar store and bought a bottle of water. She came back and she walked right up to the lead preacher and said, 'Sir, in my religion, the Quran teaches us to welcome the stranger. So, welcome to Dearborn. I can imagine on this very hot day that your mouth must be very dry from all your preaching. Here, have this water.' He took the water and looked at her, dumbfounded into silence for a bit. I have to believe this act will haunt him for the rest of his life. Her demonstration was bold, active, creative and it was nonviolent. It was absolutely amazing. It is what this work is about. Love wins. We are sowing seeds for the future.* (5)

Kim is often challenged by what to call herself and this work. *"The word 'peace' can be used to maintain an unjust status quo and avoid the hard work of justice. Peace for whom?"* (6) When we use the word "peace," it usually means something else is really present, keeping it from being realized. It seems justice is needed for all before there can be any peace. So, are we peacemakers, peace-keepers, peace space makers, justice-makers? As she ponders these labels, I am reminded of the work of the Reverend Gregory Boyle and the Homeboys Industries. Located in Los Angeles, the organization is a place for young people who have been incarcerated, have been in gangs, have been addicted to drugs, or struggle with homelessness. These young people are offered a different solution in the form of work. Homeboy Industries employs anyone interested in leaving their previous life of destruction in order to participate in an eighteen-month rehabilitation and re-entry program by working in various jobs. They work on themselves with therapy, education, substance abuse treatment and job training. In his book, *Barking to the Choir,* [7] Boyle says kinship comes before justice. We need to see each other as kin, or we will never be able to sit at the table and have a discussion. If we connect to our kinship first, then we feel the importance of justice for all. When we have this connection, peace is the byproduct.

Kim was a teacher at Holy Redeemer High School in Detroit prior to moving to University of Detroit Jesuit High School. Holy Redeemer High School was subsequently closed, leaving only two Catholic high schools in the city, both of them were all-boys institutions. Believing there should be a Catholic high school for girls in the area, the nuns of the Immaculate Heart of Mary and many others committed to issues of justice established the co-educational Cristo Rey High School on Vernor Street. Kim's daughter is now a teacher at Cristo Rey.

All the students come from low-income families and earn their tuition. One day a week, students go to various businesses in the community and work for the entire day, then the business pays their tuition to the school. Partnerships have been established in various small and large businesses, in health care venues and at universities in the area. Students work in a job-sharing plan, with each day of the week being covered by a different student at the job site. The Cristo Rey motto is "The School That Works."

Kinship is a regularly supported value fostered at Cristo Rey High School. Before classes start in the fall, there is a full week of orientation for the incoming freshman class where they learn the job-sharing arrangement and their responsibilities for assigned roles. The Meta Peace Team has been asked to provide a half-day of Nonviolence Skills Training to the students during their orientation week. By the fall of 2018, the peace team had been conducting training for four years. *So now every student in the school has had our training.* [8]

I participated as an MPT trainer at Cristo Rey High School in 2018. The training is set up in four rooms, each with a different focus lesson. Students rotate between the rooms, receiving all four lessons by lunchtime. In 2018, I was paired with Dorothy Aldridge, an African American woman in her mid-80s who is an iconic activist in Detroit. She is an MPT trainer who was part of the civil rights movement working to help citizens in the South register to vote in the 1960s. She showed students a documentary film titled "Mighty Times: The Children's March" produced by Teaching Tolerance. The film focuses on the civil disobedience of what was known at the time as "D-Day"; when the children of Birmingham, Alabama, took to the streets for civil rights in 1963. The iconic pictures of fire hoses and police dogs biting nonviolent children marching for their civil rights has often been cited as a turning point in the movement. It is a story of empowerment for the students to use their voice, their hands, and their feet for issues of justice.

In the second room, Kim Redigan presented the "Continuum of Violence." Similar to the lesson presented in an eight-hour MPT training, it was an interactive discussion regarding "what is violent," and "what is nonviolent." Where do we stand along the continuum when it comes to incidents that could be perceived as violent or nonviolent — such as using racist or sexist slurs when talking about someone, throwing wrappers from a fast food meal out the car window, experimenting on animals, pushing someone into sexual activity after refusal, spray painting graffiti on a building that is hosting a hate group, bullying someone on the Internet, excluding someone because of their race, sexual orientation, or income. As the students explained their positions, the others were allowed to change their own position by moving one way or another along the continuum, after hearing different perspectives from their classmates. Rather than a binary definition of right or wrong, the lesson illustrated that there are many gray areas. The continuum exercise stimulates thoughtful reflection for all involved.

In the third room, Sister Liz Walters and Sister Nancy Ayotte with the IHM order presented the Spirituality of Nonviolence. Their lesson included discussions in how to stay centered in values, priorities, and an inner wisdom as the students face the windstorm of life in their adolescence. Not only are there global issues such as climate change, poverty, income inequality, racism and sexism as challenges of our time, but students also face the pressures of identity and sexual development, family and friend issues, social media, and personal goal-setting. Connecting with peers and teachers broadens their social support network as they navigate the often stormy waters of adolescence.

The fourth room hosted local artists who had a project for the students. The summer of 2018 saw a great deal of debate and struggle for immigrants and families seeking asylum from violence and poverty in their home countries of Honduras, Guatemala, and El Salvador. Many families have been housed in tent cities at the border, awaiting processing as American government officials argue over walls and homeland security. Most of the students in the school are Latinx or African-American, and their own family stories align with the children at the border. Students were given the supplies to make decorative cards for the immigrant children, with statements of hope and well wishes for their journey. Applying colorful markers, yarn, buttons, and a bit of bling, students wrote messages to children unknown to them, but known on some deep level. Kim, with tears in her eyes, ooh-ed and aah-ed over the completed cards and the outpouring of love and support from these 14- and 15-year-olds.

One hundred percent of the students at Cristo Rey High School go on to college. Their work sites often provide paid summer internships or jobs while they attain further education. The school is a community and has created a culture of kinship. When there is kinship with each other, there is a desire for justice for all our kin, and where there is justice there is peace.

As a teacher at the University of Detroit Jesuit High School, Kim uses her summer break as a time for activism. The summer of 2018 saw demonstrations and civil disobedient actions for the Poor People's Campaign as organized by Reverend William J. Barber and Reverend Liz Theoharis. It was a broad call for a moral revival to end systemic racism, poverty, militarism, environmental destruction and other injustices, while trying to build a just, sustainable and participatory community. Across the country, there were large networks of people who gathered weekly for six weeks, focusing on these different issues affecting all of us, especially the most vulnerable. The organizers of the Michigan Poor People's Campaign contacted the Meta Peace Team, and together they provided trainings across the state for various groups. The trainings had many role plays for Bystander Intervention and civil disobedience. They utilized "hassle lines," to practice the skills of CLARA (Centering, Listening, Affirming, Responding, and Adding Information). People stood in lines facing each other, paired with someone in the other line. Each was given a role to play, escalating over a defined issue in order to practice the skills of centering, listening, and affirming. Many of the "hypothetical" role plays were opportunities to practice the skills that would be needed in the proposed actions for each week of the movement.

Every Monday afternoon for six weeks, close to a thousand people gathered at a church parking lot in downtown Lansing, and marched with signs and singing to the steps of the State Capitol. There were speakers each week, then the Poor People's Campaign members would proceed with their weekly "Action." Each week, the Meta Peace Team fielded a team of eight to ten people.

The issue of poverty was the theme for the first week of the Poor People's Campaign. Along with thousands of people from the state, there were many religious leaders including ministers, priests, rabbis, and imams. It was a joyous event as the Meta Peace Team walked alongside participants, monitoring the area for any potential violent escalation. The action of the week was the occupation of the street in front of the Capitol, essentially blocking all traffic. It was done in a peaceful manner, and the police presence stood by in a guarded manner but did not try to intervene or stop the action. The presence of the people was the statement in and of itself.

The theme of the second week was health and human service. Again, the crowds gathered and marched, accompanied by the Meta Peace Team, whose goal with their presence was not as a participant in the march, but to de-escalate any potential violence from wherever it could originate, including law enforcement. The action of the Poor People's Campaign members, who had been specifically trained in tactics and responses involved in civil disobedience, was to block the four entrances of the Health and Human Services Building in downtown Lansing. Members of MPT were present at each door. There were 17 arrests that day, but each arrest was done in a calm, nonviolent way. It is not the goal of MPT to be rid of conflict, but to be a presence in the conflict so it doesn't escalate into violence. The members of the PPC had a message to send with their action, and the police had their job to do in keeping the doors to the building safely open. Both sides accomplished their work and were able to do so in a nonviolent way.

I was on the peace team during Week Three, with its theme of militarism. It was a warm sunny day in late May, with people of all ages and races marching to the steps of the Capitol. There were moms and dads pushing strollers, elders walking with canes, many holding signs, *"Arms are for hugging"* and statements about the billions of dollars spent on the military industrial complex rather than on human services. As the speakers came to the podium on the Capitol steps, the peace team stood on the periphery of the crowd, keeping watch. At one point, a police officer on a bicycle approached and asked what type of action had been planned. We had been instructed to withhold this information if anyone asked, in order that the action proceed organically. I referred the officer to the police liaison of the Michigan PPC on the podium. He rode away without his desired answer.

When the speakers were completed, the thirty or so members of the PPC leadership team walked in silence to the lawn of the State Capitol and placed white wooden crosses and black wooden coffins onto the ground, signifying millions of lives lost during the military actions of our country and others. Ministers sang prayers over the coffins. Then the team and the crowd marched in an organized fashion into the Rotunda of the Michigan State Capitol, with its ornate marble columns, tile mosaics and domed ceiling. On the floor in the Rotunda, the leadership team held a "die-in," where the members lay on the floor as if they were dead. Supporters from the crowd walked around the circular gathering of those in the "die-in," singing songs of peace, possibility and wisdom. Standing on the edge of the crowd as part of the peace team, I was awed at the reverence of those lying on the ground, those walking around them and the members of the police who stood on guard from the second floor looking down at the action below. As the building was closed for the evening, those in the "die-in" were peacefully arrested for not leaving the building. Again, the witnessing presence of a peace team changed the tone, and conflictual interactions did not escalate to violence.

Rather than being a part of the peace team, Kim participated in the action for the fourth week, given the theme of water safety. Feeling compelled to use her voice in protest of the inequities regarding access to clean water, Kim chose to participate rather than take a neutral stance as a peace team member. Surrounded by the Great Lakes, Michigan is deeply affected by issues of water supply and safety. The action of the Poor People's Campaign members was a celebration of the four directions and the beautiful state of Michigan. There was a presence of PPC members at each of the four entrances to the Michigan Department of Environmental Quality building, wrapping crime tape around the doors and blocking the entrances. The north door represented the struggles with the Enbridge-owned natural gas Line 5 and the risk it poses. A rupture would seriously damage the Great Lakes. The east door represented Flint, Michigan; given the lead in the drinking water and the deaths from Legionnaires disease, a crisis brought about when the emergency manager appointed by then Governor Rick Snyder switched the city's water supply to a contaminated water supply. The south door represented Detroit and issues with the Detroit River, and contamination of the waters in the area. The west door represented Grand Rapids, noting the emerging issues with P-FAS (polyfluoroalkyl substances) contamination of ground water and how to detoxify this risk for multiple communities in Michigan. Kim said,

*I was part of the action, so I wasn't on a peace team for this issue. I needed to march. I needed to be a part of this from the protester perspective. So I didn't wear the peace team vest that day. But I was proud to watch the members of the Meta Peace Team do*

*their work. It was inspiring. I was arrested that day, but it was peaceful and purposeful. And MPT was a real presence to help make it so.* [9]

Week Five saw an action by and for the Fast Food Workers union, who brought their own peacekeeper team, so MPT was not asked to be a presence. Then Week Six was held in downtown Detroit, regarding the issue of gentrification. Thousands of people gathered at the fountain in the Campus Martius area in Detroit, addressing the struggles between money infused into the rebuilding of downtown Detroit and the displacement of thousands of low-income households with those changes. Much of the demise of Detroit is attributed to the loss of the tax base, as businesses and people moved out of the city and into the suburbs. The newly constructed "Q-line" carries commuters from one wealthy downtown area to another, and is a symbol of the gentrification problem of many inner cities. The action of the PPC members included carrying buckets of water from the fountain and blocking the entrance to the Q-line for transportation. MPT was a presence that hot June day, staying on the periphery but ready for any violence de-escalation needed. Thankfully, the protesters arrested that day were not treated violently, given the effect of the peace team.

Kim has learned from her work over the years and is a role model for many. She has learned how to sit with injustice, with disparity, and the righteous anger she feels about many issues in her community, including water safety, poverty, racism, and income inequality.

She has also come to understand that her ability to quickly move to a place of nonviolence comes from years of training, practicing, and embracing a philosophy of nonviolence while at the same time respecting others who do not agree.

*We have to be careful to not impose our nonviolence onto someone else. It is not my place to tell others how to resist.* [10]

It is a delicate dance between being and doing. Can we be a presence with someone "where they are," and not impose "where we are" onto them? Can we allow them to be heard, and allow them their own solutions? Again, it is the push and pull of America. In this space of tension, organizations like the Meta Peace team can be a presence allowing the conflict, supporting each variant side to find their answers. Kim acknowledges:

*The hardest thing for me as a human doing this work centered around grievous injustices, is when I allow myself to not be governed by my best light. I don't want to be a "white savior" that swoops in and tries to change things. I think the hallmark of this work is to have humility, to stand back, and let others lead. To model solidarity and accountability. We need to be respectful and stay centered. Violence is easy; it does not require creativity. But the tools of nonviolence are many, offering many tactics and options and this can be daunting at times. Nonviolence is harder than resorting to violence. So, we use the tools of Active Nonviolence to be a space maker for peace.* [12]

We can be active, bold, creative and nonviolent in our responses to challenging situations. It takes great courage, great patience, and great teachers. Kim, like the people of the Meta Peace Team, are trying to fill that role.

*Sheri Wander at a Meta Peace Team training, reviewing the Cage of Oppression*

## CHAPTER FIVE

# OPENING THE WINDOWS

*It is important to work toward authenticity in relationships across differences. Authenticity is based on trust, honesty, genuineness, responsibility to each other, willingness to be open and humble, willingness to take risks, and the understanding that tension in the relationship is a necessary component that will lead to growth. —Dionardo Pizaña*

Early November in Michigan is typically greeted with falling orange, red and yellow leaves as the last ones finally lose their grip on the branches. The swirling wind scatters them to yards away from their own. Some of these leaves gather by the chain link fence around a small front yard, with a gate at the sidewalk. The sign on the fence invites people to come and sit on the Adirondack chairs in the yard and read a book from the lending library in the corner of the enclosure. On the front porch, pumpkins sit on the table beside the glider, a resting place for a lounging plastic skeleton — remnants of a Halloween celebration. A rainbow-colored flag with a peace sign hangs on the side of the house. I knock on the door.

Sheri Wander welcomes me into the warm home, where she introduces me to a few of the residents who are there for the evening. The house is fashioned on the Catholic Worker House model, where people from the community can come and go for respite, shelter, food and family. There are boundaries and rules; of which the community is aware their welcome would be extinguished if not followed. The house opens into the living room, painted a warm maroon, with two couches and a kitchen table with chairs. This area extends into the large kitchen, where tall cupboards reach to the ceiling, each labeled with its contents. Off the kitchen are stairs that lead to the basement where there are sections allotted for clothing, shelves of shoes and boots, an area for food, a place for household items, and a laundry space. People can come and do their own laundry or go "shopping" in the various areas for supplies, all of which are donated.

The community mostly consists of people who are homeless, or those transitioning from one place to another. Some of the people in the community have mental health issues, drug issues, or find themselves between paychecks or jobs and need support to get back on their feet. The Peace House, as it is known, is designed for short term stays, as a bridge to something else. There are strict boundaries because *sometimes people would come and never leave.*" But this is not healthy for the person or for the Peace House. On any given night, there are usually three to four people who stay, along with Sheri who lives there permanently. Sheri's "street name" is "Mom," and over the years, she has had to learn the gentle art of saying "no" while also contributing what she can for the health of those she serves.

We return to the first floor and off to the right of the living room, a small hallway leads to two bedrooms and the bathroom. On the brightly colored walls, there are "preachy postcards" with all sorts of empowering statements. The bedroom on the left has two single beds, with yellow walls and an orange set of drawers, exuding happiness and joy. The bedroom on the right has one single bed, and another round kitchen table with chairs. The walls are lime green, and there is art work on the table from a previous activity. The storage closet on the side of the room is covered with a flowing light curtain to separate the business from the art. It seems there was much thought put into each space, each color placed on the wall, and each statement presented in a frame.

We make ourselves comfortable at the table, and Sheri tells me her Peace House work is congruent with her Meta Peace Team work. Having graduated from Kent State with a degree in Peace Studies, Sheri consciously applies her interests and skills in conflict management and nonviolent interventions to de-escalate tension in her work and in her relationships.

*For me, the Peace House is the same work as MPT. We are building a different world. I think we can do this without militaries, and violence and a militarized police force, if we can create peace with nonviolent interventions. I believe we can care for one another, the way I believe that whatever power got us here, whether you call it God or something else, calls us to take care of one another. We know how to do that. But we set up these top-down institutions where we don't take care of each other, we 'other-ize' each other and throw bread crumbs and expect people to be okay, then tell them it is their fault if they can't make it. So, this is an alternative to make the world a different place. It is about mutual aid.* [1]

Many organizations and groups work to this end. I think of Habitat for Humanity building homes for low-income families who put their own sweat equity into the building alongside people, like my parents, who volunteer to make it possible. I think of the Michigan Citizens for Prison Reform, which is a grassroots family-led initiative assisting families with loved ones in the correctional system. Programs like Homeboys Industries in Los Angeles provide rehabilitation and re-entry for people leaving gangs. The Peace House works with many in the marginalized communities in her city. Because of the sharper demarcation between "us" and "them," we are presented with a challenge to get back to our kinship with each other.

With so many examples of this separation, I ask her to explain a model called the "Cage of Oppression." Having worked with Sheri in trainings for the Meta Peace Team, I have appreciated how she uses this model to explain privilege and our perceived separation from each other. The Cage of Oppression was originally defined by Marilyn Frye, an American philosopher and feminist theorist, who studied the moral psychology of social categories such as racism, sexism, white supremacy and the marginalization of gays and lesbians. She uses the image of the bars of a birdcage coming down to trap those inside with each bar fitting together to form the cage. The bars are racism, sexism, classism, ageism/adultism, able-ism, heterosexualism, anti-Semitism, and lookism. [2] Often, we see only the bar in front of us, but if we take a broader view, we can see there are multiple bars that make up the cage and trap us. Marilyn Frye states:

> It seems sometimes that people take a deliberately myopic view and fill their eyes with things seen microscopically in order not to see macroscopically. [3]

Sheri learned of the Cage of Oppression from a group called Cultural Bridges, and a woman named Jonah, who further described two floors in the birdcage. On the top floor are the privileged, the non-targeted or valued identities. On the floor below are the non-privileged, the targeted or non-valued identities. The different bars of oppression trap us all, but those on the top floor are not aware of those on the bottom floor. However, those on the bottom floor are definitely aware of what is happening on the floor above them. It is an illustration of privilege, with those valued identities on the upper floor not even realizing how their actions affect the non-valued identities or targeted identities on the lower floor.

Some people have identities from both the top and the bottom floors, which is an example of inter-sectionality. A white male is typically in the valued identity group, but if he is gay, then this identity is typically considered a non-valued group, placing him on the bottom floor. A white educated female is typically in the valued identity group, but if she is obese, then she is typically treated as those in the non-valued group, placing her on the bottom floor. The Cage of Oppression starts a discussion, a conversation about issues and privilege and the responsibility all of us in the cage have with one another to dismantle it.

The model also gives those in the training an opportunity to be aware of our own identities and histories. It is sometimes hard to own these identities and realize the effect of privilege on our lives. But it is important to understand and be aware of these identities and how we affect or are affected by them. This tool gives people an opportunity to evaluate; how does privilege allow us the chance to do this work, and how does it get in the way of this work? When working on a peace team, or participating in a Bystander Intervention, instead of rushing in to "save the day," which adds another layer of disempowerment, we can stand in solidarity and allow them their own sense of agency.

As an illustration of her stark introduction to understanding privilege and the Cage of Oppression first hand, Sheri tells a few stories from her peace team work in Palestine. The first time she went to the area in 2001, it was to do Nonviolence Skills Training. Her affinity team consisted of two African American men from Boston, and one Palestinian American woman from New York. They were staying in the home of a Palestinian family whose home was scheduled to be demolished by the Israeli soldiers. Typically, the peace team would ask the family how they can best be of service, with some families asking for a witness as their home is demolished, or for help in moving their belongings, or to stay and help protect their home from demolition, which is often arbitrarily decided by Israeli soldiers. In the meeting with their host family, the head of the household asked the peace team to be with them when the Israeli soldiers came to demolish their home so he could tell them *"I will not let you enter my home, and we are not leaving."* One of the men on her affinity team looked directly at Sheri and said:

*Well, if the soldiers knock on the door, it is your lily white ass that's going to answer the door, because I don't look all that different from the people here.* [4]

Sheri admits to the horrifying realization in that moment when she understood it was her white skinned privileges keeping herself and this family safe.

*For the first time in my life, I realized what being white meant and the role privilege plays in the world.* [5]

In 2003, Sheri returned to Palestine to work with the International Solidarity Movement (ISM) and their affinity peace team was assigned to the city of Tulkarem. Nearly every day, the Israeli soldiers would declare a curfew, and the children would have to leave school early while businesses closed to honor the curfew. If they didn't honor the curfew, there would be a price of violence to pay. In retaliation, the older children would throw rocks or bottles or Molotov cocktails at the armored tanks and vehicles driven by the Israeli soldiers through the streets of their town. Soldiers would respond with tear gas, rubber bullets and if no internationals were present, there might be live ammunition. The role of the peace team was to help escort the youngest children through the maze of violence to get them home safely to their parents. It was a routine dance of violence, with each side playing their part, and every few days it would be the same thing time and again.

Sheri found herself getting annoyed at the older kids throwing rocks. Clearly their violence paled in comparison to the occupying forces of Israeli soldiers, and Sheri felt annoyed with herself for being annoyed at the kids. She felt like screaming, *"Don't you see you feed into their dance of violence with your action!"* Finally, through an interpreter, Sheri asked the older kids:

*Why do you throw rocks and bottles? Don't you see the soldiers are just messing with you? They just want you to respond and you do so by throwing things back at them. I am curious, what are you hoping to get out of it?*

The kids responded:

*These are our streets, and they don't have a right to be here. It is not a border town. They are coming into our streets and we need to let them know they have no right to be here.* [6]

Then Sheri asked them if there were other ways they could communicate or show the soldiers they were not welcome in their tanks and armored vehicles. The kids came up with a plan to sit on the street and asked the ISM peace team to sit with them. That day, the Israeli soldiers did not come down their street. The kids felt a real sense of empowerment and victory. As the ISM peace team processed this with the kids, Sheri recalls hearing the coordinator tell the kids that in the future, they were not to sit alone in the street without a peace team present to witness. It became evident to Sheri that the presence of their white skin and their American privilege needed to be present for this to work, and that message was being reinforced for those children. She felt awful, but she knew it was true. It was another lesson in white privilege and how it affects the world.

*It made me really think on this and weigh this idea of privilege. For me, it is really important that we don't reinforce this. But the only way to not reinforce white supremacy and U.S. colonialism is to be constantly vigilant to it, constantly question our motives and constantly examine our privilege, to examine the way that privilege allows us to do this work. And how privilege can get in the way of this work as well.* [7]

Sheri puts the Cage of Oppression in the context of her values, feeling strongly that her actions need to be nonviolent with what she calls "tone-policing," a constant effort at not sounding or being judgmental about the values of people who may feel different. It is often an effort to avoid sounding condescending, because when we take this tone, people fight back or respond with anger as their agency feels under attack or controlled. I share a story of an early lesson from my life about agency. When our son, Aaron, was about 4 years old, he refused to flush the toilet after using it. As he became more adamant about not flushing the toilet, my husband and I decided to pull back and stop pushing. We went about our day and a little while later, Aaron asked my husband to do something for him. My husband responded that he would help him, but asked if he had flushed the toilet yet. Aaron thought about this for a minute, then politely instructed us to go into the backyard and leave the house for a bit. When he welcomed us back into the house, we noticed the toilet had been flushed. My husband helped him with his request, and we all went on with our day. It was a stark lesson about Aaron's need for agency and the ability to save face. As his parents, we learned early-on how important it was for us to allow him his space and his say, rather than controlling and imposing our privilege and position onto him. The Cage of Oppression helps us understand how the oppressed or marginalized can feel trapped without a way out, and how this can lead to potentially regrettable consequences. The perception of a lack of agency leads to feelings of disempowerment and this then often becomes the root of violence.

When I think of the Cage of Oppression, I imagine an animal pacing in a metal cage. I can imagine the trapped feeling leading to scratching, growling, biting. I imagine this same feeling in the marginalized communities in inner cities, in poverty. After Michael Brown was killed by police in Ferguson, Missouri, in August 2014, the angry reaction erupted into fires, vandalism and riots. Some of the privileged white news organizations focused on the mayhem created by the black and brown people protesting and rioting in their own streets. What these news organizations failed to tell is the story of decades of oppression by the white police force; the tickets handed out to black drivers disproportionately more so than to their white counterparts, with monies collected amounting to 32 percent of the revenue for the city of Ferguson and was an actual line item in their budget. There was systematic jailing of black people for minor infractions, and a culture of police brutality particularly toward black and brown people. The cage was getting tighter and tighter and the killing of Michael Brown was the straw that broke the camel's back.

Trauma hurts people in ways that continue the cycle of violence. According to Danielle Sered, executive director of Common Justice, there are four core drivers of violence: shame, isolation, exposure to violence, and the inability to meet one's economic needs. [8] These are the screws that tighten the Cage of Oppression and often push people to the point of committing violence. These core drivers are part of institutional violence which fuels the cycle of violence with racism, economic disparity, sexism, homophobia, anti-Semitism. As in Ferguson, the smoldering heat of oppression resulted in counter violence — riots, crime, revolts. The violent response of the state or the police then causes more repression of the oppressed, which is a continuation of institutional violence. It is a sick cycle repeated time and again.

This was illustrated for Sheri while in Palestine living with the family whose home was scheduled for demolition. Sheri recalls sitting around talking with the family, and getting to know more of their story. Their son, without their knowledge or consent, had become a suicide bomber. By the time they learned of his radicalization, it was too late to save him. One night, he simply did not come home. That's when they knew. He had died carrying out his mission, and for that reason, the family home was slated for demolition. Violence begets violence. The son had been angered by the violent treatment from the Israeli military toward his people, and became violent in reaction to it. Now, further reactive violence was planned in the demolition of his family's home.

The peace team was providing Protective Accompaniment for the family and one evening, there was a loud explosion. They soon realized a home in the refugee camp had been blown up. After calling around, they were relieved to know their fellow peace team friends were safe, while also feeling horrified that someone's house had been ruined. Feeling shaken by the experience, it was difficult to fall asleep that night. Another explosion shook the house and woke everyone from their troubled sleep. Another house had been demolished. This happened another two or three times that night. It occurred to Sheri that the son who had chosen to become a suicide bomber had experienced many nights like this and must have felt this was his only recourse, to retaliate and fight back. Sheri remembers thinking that she could not guarantee that she herself would not resort to such action given the same experience. Facing the feeling of violence within herself was "scary and depressing." It became evident that the trapped feeling of those marginalized by the Cage of Oppression, and stuck in the cycle of violence often use violence as their only perceived response to the cage. Those with privilege would do well to understand this response and work on dismantling the cage with the building of agency in all its members.

While her evenings are spent at the Peace House, hosting members of the community and arranging various activities such as book nights, health education activities, art expression, movie nights and the recent Halloween party, Sheri spends her days at the Daytime Warming Center. It is a place where people from the community find respite from the streets. At Peace House, Sheri finds daily opportunities to use her MPT skills of CLARA — Centering, Listening and Affirming. If a respectful connection is made, then she can Respond and even Add information or feedback to the interchange. She tries to include daily lessons for the community in the skills of listening, conflict resolution, and tension de-escalation.

One day, an argument broke out between a man and a woman as they approached the Warming Center. The man was yelling and berating the woman, and a Warming Center worker named John interrupted him:

*Hey, man, leave her alone. Clearly she wants to be away from you, so back off.*

John's forceful interaction enraged the man even more, and he turned his attention from the woman to John and followed him into the Warming Center. Sheri was there and started to interact with the irate man, using the techniques of CLARA, while her co-worker, Brandi, turned her focus on John in an attempt to calm him as well.

In the meantime, the twenty people from the community who were at the Warming Center that morning got up and stood together, forming a wall between the fighting men. Apparently, they had been listening to those lessons.

The ruckus had also awakened Gladys, who had been sleeping on the floor. Gladys has been diagnosed with schizophrenia and probable multiple personality disorder. When she was startled awake, she started screaming, which was not unusual for her. But then a strange thing happened. She looked over at the confrontation, and once she realized what was happening, she walked over to the irate man and gently placed her hand on his arm and in a quiet voice said: *"Young man, this is not how we behave here."* Everyone stopped and just looked at her. It was an amazing day.

———

One never knows what effect we have on others, how our words or our role modeling will become food for thought and potential change in the future. Sheri realized that day at the Warming Center how important it was to continue the daily lessons on nonviolence and Active Listening.

She recalled another story, this one from the Pride Rally in Lansing, Michigan. For a number of years, the Meta Peace Team has been invited to attend the rally and the march, which culminates at a downtown park at the river's edge. Typically, the march is a joyous affair with music and dancing and the waving of multicolor flags. For some, it is a time when holding the hand of a partner in public is safe and welcomed, and they can celebrate who they are and whom they love. But every year, at the same corner, the same group of evangelical preachers gathers, holding their same inflammatory signs.

Sheri recognized a young preacher from the previous year. At that time, he had no sign, but this year he held one. It read: *"Jesus hates sin."* It wasn't a personal message of hate, like the others, just a general statement. She noticed how quiet he was, so she approached him.

*You look like you're enjoying this about as much as I am.*

The minister looked at Sheri and admitted,

*This is the part of our ministry that is hardest for me. I really don't like doing this.*

His response prompted Sheri to use her skills with CLARA, by asking more questions to further understand him and any commonality she could find with him.

*So why are you here? Is it because you believe you are going to change anyone, or change hearts and minds of anyone and someone won't be queer tomorrow? I am an activist and I participate in marches and protests because I believe we can speak truth to power and change hearts and minds by our actions. Sometimes we do and sometimes we don't. Sometimes it is just about unmasking power. So, I am curious, why are you here?* [9]

The minister replied:

*My job is to speak the truth and let Jesus change the hearts and minds. We believe God wants us to say this. We have different truths.* [10]

Sheri responded with an affirmation in their common ground, each trying to speak truth as they understood it, while noting that they had different understandings of those truths. They continued to talk for a while. When it came time for the preachers to leave, Sheri and others started escorting the preachers to their vehicles with Protective Accompaniment, given the tension they created with their inflammatory slogans and judgmental tone. Sheri caught up with the young preacher, feeling she had established a relationship of respect by listening and affirming their commonality. She then proceeded into the "R" in CLARA, which is Responding when she told him:

*I appreciate talking with you today, but I just want you to know that what you said today hurts me. I identify as queer, bisexual, and I feel hurt by your words today. They make me want to turn away from Christianity because I don't want to be associ-*

*ated with a religion or a belief system that hurts people. I would rather be a part of a belief system that has my back and wants to protect people. That's why I am here today in this Protective Accompaniment role. Your words hurt me today, because my faith is important to me, too.* [11]

The young preacher paused and said:

*I'm so sorry you were hurt by our words today.*

He said he could see her faith was important to her because she was there today to help protect them. Sheri could see in his face, in his misting eyes, that he understood. She felt that there had been a breakthrough in understanding and affirmation in their shared humanity. Another preacher in the group must have seen this too, and quickly came over and took his arm, letting Sheri know they were close enough to their cars and would no longer be needing her accompaniment. The young preacher was pulled away. But Sheri will never forget the look on his face. It was a moment where they were really human with each other, a true alignment. Sheri does not recall seeing him at the rally the following year.

Typically at the Pride Rally, there is a sort of "Bible Jeopardy," where members from the Pride march and members of the preacher group yell their perceived supporting Bible verses back and forth at each other. This was going on in earnest and a young man from the Pride group talked with Sheri. He told her:

*I'm really glad this group is here (referring to the yelling ministers). It gives these young people a chance to yell back. There isn't any violence, just a place to yell back. I can't yell at my whole family but there is a space here to give voice to the anger and the hurt. This is a place to give back my pain.* [12]

Often, gay people don't feel able to be themselves, and having a space to put this anger and hurt in a nonviolent way may prevent violence further down the road. It felt empowering to Sheri to be able to support this space of vulnerability and courage with the work of the Meta Peace Team.

The hospitality work of the Peace House and the nonviolent work of the Meta Peace Team involves learning to be comfortable in your own discomfort. It is learning to live in the gray zone because nothing is black or white. It is living the contradictions, which is often a challenge to do so and feel comfortable with that contradiction. Can we see the humanity in the preacher who has labeled us a sinner? Can we see the fear and fatigue in the eyes of the Palestinian youth who throw rocks, and for that matter, in the Israeli soldiers who drive the bulldozers over their homes? Can we see and acknowledge that there are abusive police but that there are also police who are amazing people who went into their profession for the same reason people go into peace team work? Seeing the individual and recognizing their humanity is living the contradictions.

Sheri illustrates this contradiction as she remembers the woman who was detoxing from heroin, alcohol and cocaine all at the same time. Lori was vomiting blood and getting so sick that Sheri thought she was going to die. She couldn't get into a treatment program to help her with the detox because of insurance issues and there wasn't room in the program. She saw this person suffering, and realizing she didn't have the medical training to help her through this, grappled with the moral dilemma of what to do to help. Sheri bought her a bottle of booze, feeling pretty sure Lori wouldn't survive going cold turkey off all the drugs at once. She was living in the gray zone.

She first met Lori a few years before, when people from the community called Sheri for help. Lori had been badly beaten by her boyfriend or her pimp. Sheri never learned who had done this to her. She found Lori curled into a ball, rocking beside the park bench in the local park. Sheri didn't know what to do, so she started by doing what's called "Up and Out" training, asking Lori questions to bring her back to the present time. She introduced herself, and asked Lori to do her a favor; tell me how many bricks you see on the bottom row of this planter? Okay, now list four things you see that are green in the plaza. These questions were meant to help bring Lori back to the moment rather than reliving the beating. Eventually Sheri was able to get Lori to the emergency room at the hospital. There, the police came in and treated Lori with disrespect, noting she deals with drugs and lives on the streets. Sheri noted she was aware of the issues, and that Lori had been beaten. After suggesting that the crime should be addressed, Sheri was threatened with arrest. She then responded:

> *Okay. You have your job to do and I have my job to do. I am choosing to help her. My job is to advocate for someone who is a victim of a crime, and I would think our jobs line up. But if they don't, I understand you have to do what you have to do.* (13)

Sheri credits the teachings from the Meta Peace Team as giving her the ability to respond in a peaceful, matter-of-fact way. Lori eventually got off heroin, although she continued to drink for some time. As of the writing of this book, Lori is finally in a three-month residential treatment program and is doing okay. Recalling her history with Lori, Sheri feels she made the best decision she could with the information she had at the time. She was living with the contradictions.

In many ways it would be much easier to sit on a board and drop money into a problem from afar. Being on the ground means you have to let the pain in. Sheri remembers accompanying a young man from the community to a mental health facility. When asked who would be listed as his emergency contact person, Sheri could sense in his pause for the answer there was no one he could name. So, Sheri quickly offered her phone number and then she could get ahold of his family if there was a need to do so. Later, as he spoke with the counselor, he was asked who Sheri was to him. He replied, *"She is the closest thing to family that I have."* At the time, they were mere acquaintances. Sitting with him, Sheri heard his life story and thought to herself that no one should have to live through what he had gone through. At the end of the day, feeling exhausted and overwhelmed, Sheri went back to the Mercy House where she was working, and sat on the couch and cried. The co-founder of the home, Peggy, told her, *"Loving is ridiculously hard work a lot of the time. It hurts so much because you love so much."* [14]

Admittedly, Sheri notes, it is letting in the pain that ultimately gives her the hope to continue to do the work she does. It is another contradiction. She recalls that as a child in grade school, she was taught what to do in case of fire or tornado, and they had drills to prepare for each. In case of fire, the windows are to be shut to keep out the oxygen so the fire dies. In case of a tornado, the windows are to be open, to let the pressure move through the building and lessen the damage that is potential from the storm. Seeing life as a storm of sorts, we need to leave the windows open to let the pressure flow through and past us.

Sheri is opening the windows.

*Elliott Adams speaking at a Veterans for Peace event*

## CHAPTER SIX

# LOOSENING THE CHAINS

*Do all you can, with what you have, in the place you are, with the time you have. —Nkosi Johnson, a 10-year-old from South Africa with AIDS who spoke at a World AIDS Conference in 1999*

Anyone who has a sibling can most likely remember times when there was fighting over space. *"She's sitting too close to me!" "He's on my side of the couch!"* Or the infamous placing of tape down the middle of the shared bedroom to demarcate "my" side from "your" side. This is silly childhood folderol, all to vie for power and position. When our own children were little and got into their bickering or fighting, my husband and I stayed united in our response to their altercations. We would repeatedly say, *"We don't care who started it, we care who ends it."* Amazingly, it took the wind out of their whining and crying and they figured it out themselves. If only it were that easy in the Middle East and other hot spots around our world. Sadly, we humans continue to place the tape down the middle of our shared space on earth and label anyone outside our tribe as "other."

I am not a historian or a political scientist, so I will not attempt to summarize the long history of conflict between Zionist Jews and Arab Muslims, but I will try to give it some context. After World War I and the fall of the Ottoman Empire, new boundaries were drawn for countries in the Middle East, including Palestine, Jordan, Iran, and Iraq. After World War II and the atrocities imparted on the Jews in the Holocaust, the nation of Israel was carved out of the land that had previously been designated as Palestine — the area between the Mediterranean Sea and the Jordan River. Israel was to serve as a homeland for the Jewish people, but the partitioning of Palestine in 1947 essentially displaced some 700,000 Palestinians. This was not done with the consent of the Palestinian people. The Arab countries declared war on the newly formed state of Israel in 1948, and the region has experienced some level of constant conflict ever since. In the Six Day War in 1967, Israel seized control of the Palestinian territories known as the Gaza Strip, the West Bank and East Jerusalem, which are now "occupied" by the Israeli military.

There have been many attempts at peace summits and repeated proposals for solutions in the region. Some have suggested a two-state solution, and others favor a single-state solution. There is serious opposition to both ideas. In 2005, a political and military group known as Hamas won elections and took control of Gaza. Hamas is widely considered a terrorist organization with caustic slogans touting "Death to Israel" and often uses violence to achieve its goal by sending rockets into neighboring Israeli settlements. All in the name of fighting for the rights of Palestinians to return to their homeland. Hamas refuses to recognize the legitimacy of the state of Israel, and Israel won't agree to a two-state solution — and the formation of the country of Palestine — unless Hamas accepts the right of Israel to exist. Another sticking point is the status of Jerusalem, considered a holy city by both Palestinians and Jews. In addition, there are Israeli settlers who live in the Palestinian areas and numerous Palestinians who live and work in Israeli areas, with many displaced people living in refugee camps. A single-state solution would have to guarantee equal rights and representation for Israelis and Palestinians — a prospect that is unpalatable to many in Israel. All of these issues are formidable challenges to any solution. In general, trying to achieve a lasting peace has been like trying to grab smoke.

As sincerely as we would like to have a clean definition of black and white, of right and wrong, this is an area fraught with gray. In America, we are told of the Israeli-Palestinian conflict primarily from the perspective of the Israelis. We know how the Jewish people were treated in the years leading up to World War II and the horror of the Holocaust. We understand their struggle for a Jewish homeland and we support them in this goal. We see the videotapes of Palestinian youth throwing rocks and the Hamas sponsored rockets being sent into the Israeli settlements. But there are many who believe Israel amplifies the problem with disproportional retaliation and its apartheid-like treatment of the Palestinian people. There are stories of terror rained upon the Palestinians by many Israelis, most often the nation's military, which is financially supported by the United States. What is unhelpful, is that often when the actions of the Israeli military or the Israeli government are called into question, a vehement backlash erupts. Critics are labeled "anti-Semitic," an accusation that essentially shuts down any discussion about the dysfunctional power dynamic between the occupying force of Israel and the occupied people of Palestine. The cycle of violence continues day after day and has affected the neighboring countries, as well as our own. For endless years, the conflict of people looking for their homeland continues. And violence begets violence. Hamas sends dozens of rockets into Tel Aviv, and Israel responds with disproportionately more bombs. Fundamentalists on both sides fuel the fire of hatred, which is passed down from generation to generation.

It is one of the ultimate paradoxes of our time, to see good and worthy people on all sides, and see heinous actions perpetrated against the perceived "other." Politically, we are trapped in the sticky spider web. We are challenged to step back and see the line between good and evil running down the middle of each person, not between people. There are loving and kind people in the Israeli tribe and loving and kind people in the Palestinian tribe. There are also decades of hurt that have affected grandparent and grandchild alike. Can we be a witness to horrors we rain down upon each other, and decide that our shared humanity is more important? Can we understand that the definition of insanity is doing the same violent thing over and over and expecting a different, more peaceful result?

Year after year in this region of conflict, there are peace teams placed from many different peace and justice groups, including the International Solidarity Movement, Christian Peacemaker Teams, Veterans for Peace, the Center for Human Rights and other members of the Nonviolent Peaceforce, a group of many organizations across the world doing nonviolent peace work. The Meta Peace Team tries to send a delegation to the West Bank for three weeks to three months at a time. The main role is to establish a nonviolent presence, in the hope of changing the dynamics of power and interaction between Palestinians and Israelis. Typically, the role of MPT is not to take sides. But it is difficult to not feel empathy for the plight of the Palestinians when the brunt of the violence is often borne by Palestinian civilians whose homes are demolished, whose olive groves are burned, whose children are spat upon, and whose peaceful protests are met with tear gas and bullets. The peace team members are a witness to what is really going on in the region, beyond the sound bites and the thirty-second video clips conveyed by American media. Part of the role is to be a voice for the voiceless once back in the United States, and share what they have witnessed. Some of their stories are captured here.

———————

The Meta Peace Team has typically gone to the West Bank on invitation by the Palestinian farmers for their work during the olive harvest. Olive trees are like family members to these farmers, sustaining the whole family for generations with food, oil, and income. So, it is both insult and injury when Israelis plow their fields under, or build walls separating the family from their groves. The Israeli military and Israeli settlers often terrorize Palestinian farmers by burning their trees, setting up checkpoints between their homes and their fields, or taunting them while they work. Some Israeli settlers set tires on fire and roll them down the hills into the fields, essentially setting the groves on fire and ruining the harvest.

In 2006, Peter Dougherty went to the West Bank with a delegation including the International Solidarity Movement. Peter and his affinity team were assigned to the field of a Palestinian farmer named Monter, after Israeli settlers had burned fifty to seventy of his olive trees just days before. The role of the peace team was for Unarmed Civilian Protection, known as Protective Accompaniment, while in the field for the harvest of his remaining trees. The Palestinians are eager for the presence of internationals, because their presence changes the tone in the area and makes a difference for their safety during the harvest. Peter recalls accompanying the farmer's son on donkey back to their homestead for food, and how thankful his father was for this presence. Walking past the Israeli settlers and the police at the checkpoints with an international reduced the potential for taunting and violence.

The sacred day of the week for Muslims is Friday, a day for family and community activities without work. It is on such days when there are demonstrations against the building of more settlement walls by the Israelis. These walls take land and housing away from Palestinians and create more housing for Israeli settlers. The Palestinians respond to these actions in various ways, which for some Palestinian youth includes throwing stones and rocks at the Israeli soldiers. The Israeli soldiers are also present for the demonstrations, often with guns, rubber bullets, and tear gas. Typically, the bullets are not real when Internationals are present.

Most of the Palestinians who gather on Friday nights come to be in solidarity with their neighbors in a nonviolent way. At first timid, the demonstrations are getting more creative and lively as a social gathering of support for each other, with a message to the world. There are prayer vigils, speeches, music, and sometimes dancing. One such gathering included the theme of building bridges, not walls. The Palestinian community gathered some of the materials that the Israelis were using to build the wall and used the plaster and metal to construct a "bridge," building themselves into it. One body connected to the next, the people themselves were the bridge. If one was arrested by the Israeli police, they all would be arrested.

These Friday evening demonstrations are often interrupted by the Israeli military, which shows up in full riot gear. It was one such Friday night in Bil'in where Peter was tear-gassed, and he relives the experience as he looks down at the floor, shaking his head.

*It was bad. I couldn't see and I couldn't breathe. I had to concentrate, having fallen down onto all fours, struggling for air. I could hear the noise and the screaming and people running. I couldn't breathe and I had to focus on saying to myself, 'I can. I can breathe.' But I had the feeling like I couldn't. I had to trust that one of my teammates would come and get me, and they did. The next day we went to the Quaryot field for the farmer named Hussein. My asthma started really reacting, and I sat below a tree struggling for my breath. Among the internationals on my team was Rabbi Arik Aschleman from Rabbis for Human Rights. He called an ambulance, which came and took me to the hospital. Rabbi Ruth stayed with me for the three hours they treated me. Then she took me to her home in Jerusalem, where I stayed with her and her family for two nights recuperating. She and her rabbi husband had two children, who made me laugh. I left them flowers on their doorstep to thank them before I left to return to the fields and the work of Protective Accompaniment.* [1]

Hebron is an especially difficult place for the Palestinians because the Israelis have a settlement in the middle of the town, and all around the outskirts of the city. The Palestinians have to walk through these areas to get to school or work and are often taunted by the Israelis. On the street named Tel'Rumaida, the Israeli settlers looking down on the street below would throw stones or spit on the children walking to school. One day, there was an emboldened Israeli settler woman and some girls throwing stones and beating on the Palestinian girls trying to go to school. The occupying Israeli military was present to witness the behavior but did nothing to stop it. MPT was called in as Protective Accompaniment, walking the children to and from school. Peter shudders with the memory of being called names like *"Nazi!"* and the threats aimed at internationals of *"We'll kill you!"* He notes: *"It was terrifying."* And the Palestinians and Israelis live with this behavior every day.

At one point, Peter spent five weeks with a delegation consisting of people from the Christian Peacemaker Team and five members from MPT. They lived on a rooftop and slept on mats on the floor in a small room. Sometimes they would go to a nearby university to protect students from the violence perpetrated there by Israeli soldiers. Some days, they would be a presence on Duboia Street, a cobblestone street on which there were many Palestinian businesses and shops. There were Israeli settlements on the outskirts of town at both ends of the street, so often there were Israelis traveling this road. Windows of Palestinian shops would be smashed every now and then, and threats of harassment were frequent. One day, Peter and his team decided he would utilize the skill of distraction with spontaneous clowning and juggling, trying to change the mood and the tone on the street. While his teammates watched for vehicles or armed guards, Peter juggled and had a makeshift clown show. The guards at the checkpoints smiled, and children were laughing and gleeful. There was an atmosphere of joy and playfulness.

On a different trip to the Gaza Strip in 2005, Peter was one of four religious men on the peace team. The state of Israel was becoming more strict with who was allowed into the area as a peace team, and more were allowed if part of a religious order. Peter and his MPT affinity team overlapped with an MPT team of four nuns, whose tour was completed. They rented an apartment in Rafa, and one Sunday morning, they were getting ready to leave to attend Catholic Mass in Gaza City. Their interpreter was with them, a young woman named Fida. Peter was in another room getting his backpack ready for the day when suddenly a tall Palestinian man came up the stairs and into their apartment. He said to one of the priests, *"Come here!"* Harry Bury, who was at the end of the table stood, trying to be cooperative. Then, another man jumped out of the hall and put a bag over Harry's head and dragged him down the stairs, shoved him into a waiting car and drove away. Luckily, Fida witnessed the whole event and was able to go to the area Palestinian police and, speaking in Arabic, she demanded they find him. She also met with Israeli soldiers and asked for help in trying to locate Harry to bring him back safely.

The tension and talking and asking for help went on for about three hours, when they received a call from Harry. He had been driven around and around to a place about five blocks away from their apartment. The kidnapper and the one guarding him told him to say into a microphone that he worked for the CIA and the Israeli military. Harry said he couldn't do that. Then they demanded he do it or they would kill him. So Harry said it word for word. They put the hood back over his head, and after a while, they took him out the door, removed the hood and disappeared. Recognizing the area, Harry was able to walk back to the apartment to his waiting comrades. Apparently, Harry's capture was made to get attention from the Palestinian Authority for the people of Rafa, whose requests for basic issues such as food and jobs were falling on deaf ears. People were angry they were not getting the results they called for from the Palestinian Authority and perhaps the voice of an International would achieve that desired attention. The Palestinian governor of the area came to visit the shaken peace team and apologized for the event. Gratefully, Harry had returned without injury, and despite their concern that his recording would be used for nefarious purposes, there was never evidence it caused any trouble.

━━━━━━━━

While at a home in Gaza, Sister Liz Walters, Mary Ann Ford, and other women from the peace team were sitting with some Palestinian women. A short distance away from the house was a large wall, with gun towers and patrolling Israeli soldiers. The women sat outside the home, telling stories and laughing out loud together. As told to Peter:

*We want to have those soldiers hear us laugh because they cannot destroy us. They haven't scared us so much that we can't feel this human emotion.*

Peter recalls visiting with a 48-year-old Palestinian woman in the West Bank, whose home was bulldozed to the ground twice by Israeli soldiers. Her husband and her son were in an Israeli jail for no known crime. The woman was staying with her sister-in-law at the time, as she was now homeless. Despite the trauma of her story, the woman exuded radiance, and Peter felt a buoyancy in her story-telling. He asked the woman, *"How can you remain positive with all this tragedy?"* The woman stopped and thought, then looked back at Peter and said:

*We must be like the mountain. The storms come and go, the rains fall, the torrents beat the mountain, and the mountain still stands.* [2]

Peter's voice catches and he becomes quiet as he collects himself. He notes this memory touches him every time. As a witness in the Palestinian/Israeli conflict, he has come to see that *"occupation is the fundamental crime in the cycle of violence, making Gaza the largest walled prison in the world."* [3] When the conquistadors came to the Americas and took the land from the Native Americans, the native people retaliated, and the conquistadors said, *"See what savages they are!"* The same process is happening in the West Bank and Gaza. Israeli settlers take the land from the Palestinian people and get upset when the Palestinian people react. Palestinians feel they have a right to defend their territory, and their families. Israelis feel they have a right to a homeland. Both sides respond with violence toward each other. Where does the cycle of violence end?

Of course, it is a complicated conflict and there are many entrenched in their separate tribes. It will take great courage and a willingness on each side to make some concessions. We don't care who started it. We care who ends it.

———

Elliott Adams is another Meta Peace Team member who has served on a number of international teams in the West Bank and Gaza. He has spent much of his time in community politics in his home state of New York. He served in the Rotary, Masonic Lodge, local school boards, and as mayor of the village where he lives. Elliott feels his time in politics has helped him understand the political process and to see that real change comes from the people. *"I can't go to the politicians and ask them to stop war. But the people rising up, stating this, the politicians will follow. It takes the people to rise up."* [4]

Elliott knows a little something about war. He was in the military and volunteered as a paratrooper in the Vietnam War. In the Army he was also stationed in Japan, Alaska, and Korea. When asked if he has any stories he would like to share about his service, about what he saw and what he did, he calmly and matter-of-factly answers, *"No."* He notes how he has gotten good at building walls around that experience and not talking about it. *"I can just say, I'm not going there."* And he doesn't, except to say:

*We are all capable of doing great things, and we are all capable of doing the most horrendous things. Any person who believes they could never do horrendous things, is kidding themselves. We have done things beyond comprehension. We have done things unjustifiable.* [5]

What Elliott does talk about is his experience with the Meta Peace Team and the various peace groups with which he has worked. Early on, he started working as a mediator with a peace group in New York, finding ways for both sides to come together to try to find a win-win in any conflict. He espouses *"the idea that in any conflict there are positions and needs, and a place where everyone's needs and positions can be met, if given the time and space. This peace group work was inspiring to me while working with individuals, but the idea came to me that maybe these ideas could work amongst nations."* [6]

So Elliott became active in the Meta Peace Team, and became a trainer in the skills of Active Listening, Third Party Nonviolent Intervention, and Unarmed Civilian Protection. He learned how to be a peace team member, realizing that where there is diversity, there will be conflict. Where there is conflict, there is often pain, but the escalation to violence does not need to be the response.

*War is just simple violence; it is not about conflict or conflict resolution. War does not create national security. Conflict is used to create war. We have to learn how to live in conflict, in a non-*

*violent way. We can keep walking the journey together in conflict and disagreement. Peace is the normalization of conflict. We can all be together in conflict as long as there is not violence. That is peace.* [7]

Elliott identifies the three divisions of areas in Palestine, drawn after the Oslo Peace Accords from 1993 to 1995, as an attempt to create peace in the Middle East. The Accords were designed for the recognition by the Palestinian Liberation Organization of the State of Israel, and the recognition by Israel of the PLO as the representative of the Palestinian people. These Accords, unfortunately, did not result in the peaceful interactions so hoped for between the government of Israel and the Palestinian Liberation Organization. However, their delineations of geography persist today.

**Area A:** has Palestinian administrative control and Palestinian security control. The government and the police are Palestinian.

**Area B:** has Palestinian administrative control and Israeli security control. The government is by the Palestinians and the police are Israeli.

**Area C:** has Israeli administrative control and Israeli security control. The government and the police are Israeli.

On a map, 70 to 80 percent of Palestine is Area C. It is difficult to travel anywhere without going through Area C. Often, the Israelis can shut down the area and create logjams in traffic and movement in the area by setting up blockades and checkpoints. Sometimes there are "flying checkpoints," which change daily without notice. Elliott has a friend who was going to school, noting his commute was typically fifteen minutes by car. But when the Israeli checkpoints were arbitrarily placed and enforced, his commute became four hours and he had to quit his studies and stay home. Time is told in terms of the blockades. The Meta Peace Team has been a presence, using their international privilege to stand and watch, witness, and document the actions of the soldiers at the checkpoints, and this can often change the dynamics of the behavior to be less oppressive if not thwarted.

Elliott remembers an incident at a bridge, which was completely blocked by soldiers due to some work on the water lines on the other side of the bridge. The line of Palestinians waiting to cross the bridge was growing as well as the tensions. Elliott approached a soldier on the bridge and pointed out to him that the security perimeter didn't need to cut off the entire bridge, and that by moving the blockade just five feet, people could then safely pass and the growing crowd could disperse. A few minutes later, without saying anything to Elliott or meeting his gaze, the soldier moved the blockade.

Another time, Elliott and his team of three were driving through a checkpoint and a soldier stopped their car. He demanded that the black woman in their team get out of the car. Elliott said, *"Excuse me, sir, but she is traveling with me."* He got into a discussion with the soldier, who subsequently forgot that he had asked the woman to get out, and eventually sent them on their way. As they were pulling away the soldier told them they *"shouldn't be in the West Bank because it's dangerous."* Those in the car wanted to tell the soldier it was dangerous because of him. He was the one with the gun.

In Area B, Israelis frequently hold military maneuvers and go into houses at will. It is terrorizing to have soldiers rush through the rooms and make their way to the roof to look out over the streets of the town with their guns in position. Elliott recalls getting the call to go to a home and stay in Protective Accompaniment with the family during one such raid. Upon arrival to the home, Elliott fought a temptation to lock the door and leave the soldiers out on the roof, but there would have been horrible consequences for the family. He could have gone out onto the roof and confronted the soldiers, but again, it would have escalated the situation. Instead, he sat with his back to the door and interacted with the family. While the family prepared tea for their guests, the soldiers came down off the roof and rustled past Elliott, ran down the stairs and were gone. They had really come to intimidate the Palestinian family and create fear. The MPT was there to witness and watch this event unfold.

Hearing stories of the daily events in the Palestinian/Israeli conflict, I wonder what role courage plays for someone who goes to the region as a peacekeeper. The poet David Whyte writes:

*Courage is a word that tempts us to think outwardly, to run bravely against opposing fire, to do something under besieging circumstances, and perhaps above all, to be seen to do it in public, to show courage; to be celebrated in story, rewarded with medals, given the accolade, but a look at its linguistic origins is to look in a more interior direction and toward its original template, the old Norman French 'coeur,' or 'heart'.* [8]

I believe Elliott goes to the region time and again because his heart is focused on peace, on nonviolence as a way to address conflict. He is focused on this goal and because he operates from the "coeur," he is not afraid. There was a time while in Gaza, Elliott found himself between the armed Israelis on one side and the Palestinians on the other side. Wearing a gas mask and an orange vest marking him as a member of the peace team, Elliott stood still in the middle of the fighting groups with his empty hands held outward.

*By simply standing there, without body armor, without a gun, I feel like I changed the dynamic. I felt as though all the Israeli soldiers were looking at me through a rifle, seeing me standing there. My standing there changed the perception of the conflict. It was no longer an open battle field. Here was a guy that was just*

*peacefully standing there. That is modeling. Eventually, the Pal-
estinians left the area, and I just stood there. Finally, the Israelis
left too. It shifted the perception of the conflict.* (9)

When I asked Elliott if he was afraid, he replied:

*Not really. I knew that everyone was looking for a way to shoot
around me, not at me. They don't want to shoot internationals,
there would be consequences if I were hurt. So I calculated and
took the risk. I did not feel at risk standing there. I stood there
exuding peace and calm. Once the smoke cleared, I took my gas
mask off. If I had left it on, it would have changed the balance.*

I tell him that I bet the soldiers looking at him through their
rifle sights will never forget him and what he did. I hope it is a lasting image in their memory. Elliott pauses and responds quietly:

*It occurs to me now when you say that, I wish someone would
have done this for me while I was in Vietnam. I think it might
have changed my mind if someone would have done this for me
in some of my situations.* (10)

————————

Finding itself attacked regularly, a large agricultural university in
Palestine called on the peace team to be a presence. The president
of the university told the peace team that the school's efforts to
educate and support students was hampered because it was dealing
with tear gas bombs being thrown through windows, and snipers
shooting at students. The peace team was given permission to stay
in the library and be a witness, to document what was happening
to the students. They were shown the tables on which the injured
students had lain until they could receive medical attention, six
students having been shot in the lower legs, and twenty-one were
treated for tear gas inhalation. Windows had been shot out. The

Israeli military had left bombs in the fields and these had to be removed with a front-end loader. The headmaster had been jailed by the Israeli military for no known reason. It turned out, there were Israeli soldiers on campus six to seven days a week, and the Israelis said the reason for this was because there was a military base on the campus.

By staying on the campus, MPT could document activities and incidents. They held "International Observer" signs to reduce the risk of the violence. One day Elliott walked around and looked into the windows of the buildings that the Israeli military said were their military base. The buildings were empty. No one had stayed there for years. They were abandoned. He figured they weren't defending anything, and there was no military base listed on the area map. The Israeli commanders were simply bringing soldiers over to the university to practice. The sniper practice started in October but ended in December, partly because of the presence of the MPT peaceful observers. Then the university went back to its mission of educating students.

During one of the trips to the West Bank, the Meta Peace Team had the role of Protective Accompaniment for some Palestinian farmers in their olive groves. They first had to pass through an Israeli checkpoint, and if their names were on the list, the farmers were allowed to proceed to their land. Elliott's name, however, was not on the list and they would not let him pass into the field with the farmers. Elliott insisted and informed them of his role on the peace team. One of the soldiers left to speak to their supervisor to get permission for Elliott to enter. While he waited, Elliott stayed engaged with the soldiers. They were 18- and 19-year-old men with boots, rifles, uniforms and a Jeep. He told them of his years in the military and where he had served. The eyes of the young soldiers brightened with respect. Elliott told them he had seen combat, and he could tell the soldiers were impressed as they yearned to do what he had done. As their conversation continued, the soldiers let Elliott touch their weapons. This was a big deal. It seemed the whole interaction changed and the balance of power shifted. Then one of the soldiers said:

*These rifles are American. The ammunition is American. These boots are American. The Jeep is American.*

Again, the interaction changed and the balance of power shifted. Elliott recalls thinking:

*How can I look at this Israeli as the bad guy? As an American, I am responsible.* [11]

The blanket support by the United States for Israel creates a huge problem in the Middle East because of the policies, not the people. There is violence perpetrated by each side, back and forth. But despite the possibility of the U.S. leveraging its military and financial support for Israel by holding them accountable to better relations, the U.S. becomes complicit in the violence perpetrated on the Palestinians. Other countries are angry at the U.S., send terror our way, and the cycle of violence continues. It is a huge dance of anger, with both sides following the same tired dance steps over and over. Elliott notes:

*I always recall the statement by Nelson Mandela; we don't want the chains loosened, we want them taken off. This always comes to mind when I am in the West Bank. I feel like when I am there, I am loosening the chains, trying to help make their life better. When I come back to America, I am working to take the chains off, by trying to change American foreign policy. We need to change the way Americans perceive the problem in Israel, to help the American people see that Israel is a deeply tribal society, it is not a democracy, it is the only nation that is allowed to occupy land. American foreign policy isn't going to change until we the people make it change. We need to help the American people know what is really happening there.* [12]

Elliott goes on to say:

*There shouldn't be the elimination of Israel, OR the absolute allowance of the terrorism from Israel. We need to have both sides abide by international law, and both sides sign a non-proliferation treaty. Our U.S. money should support them to be peaceful rather than violent. So far, our U.S. money helps support the Israelis in crushing the Palestinians.* [13]

If we change how we have done things, then they will have to change how they do things. This is the only way the dance of anger and cycle of violence will change. Having seen the realities of war up close and personal, both in Vietnam and in the Middle East, Elliott is impassioned about the need to end it.

*I can't make the problem go away, I can only do what I can do. I can call it what it is. I can say, 'I am great except for the fact that I live in a war culture' whenever I am greeted. It is one thing I can do. It is an attempt to educate and be aware.* [14]

Elliott sums it up this way:

*Democracy is our responsibility. I am part of the process. It matters what I do and how I vote. It doesn't have to be a big splash, not everyone will be an Olympian. But we can do what we can do. If in the morning, I decide that I am going to work to make our society better, and the sum total of us chooses this, then the world will be an ever so slightly better place. If, however, I choose to take a 'bye' day, and not do all I can do, then at the end of the day, society will be ever so imperceptibly worse and we have much work to do. We have to show up.* [15]

*An Israel settlement separated by walls and barbed wire as seen by the Meta Peace Team on a trip to the region in 2005*

## CHAPTER SEVEN

# WITNESSING

*War may sometimes be a necessary evil, but no matter how necessary, it is always an evil, not a good. We will not learn to live together in peace by killing each other's children. —Jimmy Carter, U.S. President 1977-1981*

April is a beautiful month in Palestine, with the air changing to spring and the greening of grasses and trees. Every Friday, there are demonstrations in Bil'in, and one such demonstration was in honor of Rachel Corrie, a young American activist with the International Solidarity Movement who a couple of years earlier, in 2003, was run over and killed by an Israeli bulldozer in the Gaza Strip as she tried to protect a Palestinian home from demolition. At that particular Friday night demonstration, Jonathan Pollick, one of the visiting internationals, had been hit full force in the face with a blast of tear gas from the Israeli soldiers who come to the demonstrations to intimidate and disperse the crowds. Jonathan had been seriously injured, and almost lost an eye. The following week, he was being discharged from the hospital and the community of Palestinians had planned an outdoor party in the village square to celebrate his release. Members of the Meta Peace Team who were working with the International Solidarity Movement peace teams were included in the celebration as well. Although the Palestinians in the area have very little, the people of Bil'in set out chairs and tables and served what they could; humus, pita bread, chicken, rice and roasted vegetables. They wanted to thank the young man for standing with them and welcome him "home."

The festivities were grand and boisterous, with music and singing and much embracing of the young man who had been injured. The village gave him an award in Yiddish, Hebrew and English. Looking around, it was like the Beloved Community as coined and envisioned by Martin Luther King Jr., with an eclectic group of celebrants; women wearing hijabs, men with beards, young people with their tattoos, and peace team members representing many countries across the world. Among the guests of peace teams was a filmmaker who was working on a documentary of the plight of the Palestinians under Israeli occupation. Tonight, the footage was of joy rather than the day-to-day struggles with the cycle of violence. However, word started to circulate there would be an arrest later that night. A 9-year-old boy who had been seen throwing stones was the target. Many times, the young boys try to defend their families. For years they have watched their fathers and grandfathers being humiliated with poor income sources, their olive trees destroyed, their homes demolished; so sometimes they throw stones to retaliate.

Rather than moving on to the next assignment, the members of the Meta Peace Team decided to stay in the community for the night. Mary Hanna was among those who stayed. She said it was in the pitch dark of night, around 3 a.m., when they heard the rumbling sound of tires on the gravel road. The soldiers were coming. Everyone from the peace team got up, grabbed their shoes, and ran for the home of the little boy. It was dark, so they linked arms with each other in case anyone fell as they moved through the night. When they arrived at the house, there were other internationals and many townspeople approaching with the same protective intent. Once the soldiers arrived at the home, they were obviously startled with the growing crowd, not expecting to be met with any opposition. Remaining linked arm to arm, the people stood with resolve, protecting the house and the family inside. The four soldiers went to their Jeeps, two in total, and charged the standing protectors, stopping just short of the team. No one moved. The Jeeps backed up. Again, the soldiers charged with their Jeeps and again, no one moved.

Feeling frustrated with the presence of so many townspeople, internationals from peace teams, and the filmmaker who was capturing footage of the midnight raid on a home to arrest a child, the soldiers retreated from the area to discuss the situation. Meanwhile, the protectors gathered to confer on their next plan for protection. The father of the boy spoke Hebrew and knew one or two words of English. The filmmaker was fluent in Hebrew, knew some English and a few Arabic words. The uncle was fluent in Arabic and Hebrew but no English. The rest of the team spoke English. This was the strategy meeting on the porch of the house in Bil'in at 3 in the morning.

A peace team member of the International Solidarity Movement noted the soldiers were simply waiting until everyone went back to bed and would most likely return. Mary and the other women of MPT decided they would stay with the family for the rest of the night in their home as Protective Accompaniment with his parents. In the household were two sons: the 9-year-old boy who threw the stones and his older brother, Rani, who had been paralyzed from the chest down due to an Israeli sniper bullet to his neck while protesting in Ramallah. Mary and her two team mates stayed in his room on floor mats, offered to them by the boys' parents. The parents slept in another room with their youngest son between them. All night, they listened. They could hear the sound of bleating goats in the distance, dogs barking a couple streets away, and the creaks and cracks of the wood building. But the sound of tires on the gravel road was not heard.

Finally, the night had passed and the sun came up. The family wanted to throw a celebration for Mary and the peace team for giving them a night of peace. Although they had very little, they wanted to share it with them to give their thanks. Going to the outdoor kitchen, the mother set to building the fire of dried goat dung, covered with rocks to make a place to cook the fresh pita bread. She had a small packet of sugar which she sprinkled on top of the pita bread, an obvious delicacy she was sharing. Mary notes:

> I knew in that moment that every cent I spent to get there had been worth it. That if I did nothing else, I had helped give them a gift they couldn't pay for. They saw beyond price. It was incredibly humbling for us. We knew the stories of the children 'arrested,' then taken by the soldiers and left alone out in the fields to find their own way home. Parents have no way to find them. This is a terrorizing activity done to the Palestinians and their children by the Israeli soldiers. It was heartbreaking to know we couldn't stay longer but the family was so grateful for that one night of peace. [1]

Mary's first international trip with the Meta Peace Team was in 2005, as part of an International peace team to the West Bank. She recalls being told it would be "life changing" and thinking it was such a trite thing to say. Once there, however, she knew it to be true.

> Before you leave, you don't have any idea or concept of what you can actually do that can make a difference. You are aware that you are only going to be there for four or six weeks, so it feels temporary, like a stop-gap measure. The people are anonymous, and you don't know who you are helping. You get there and you see people that just living is their act of rebellion. By not losing hope, they are fighting the system. [2]

The soldiers did not come back for the little boy. His big brother, Rani, continues to work in the peace movement as best he can.

The family is still fighting to save their orchards and protect their land. Mary heard it often from many of the Palestinian families with whom she worked, *"Please tell them, we are not terrorists."* An important role of the peace team is that of witness, to tell the stories of real families and give voice to their plight. The telling of their stories can potentially break the stereotypes fed by biased media and political decision-makers. Political policies affect real people and have real consequences.

While in the region, Mary noted the many walls that have been arbitrarily placed. After World War II, European countries without consulting Palestine gave 55 percent of the land and water to the Israelis, despite the fact they were only 35 percent of the population. The West Bank is now surrounded by Israeli territory, and the Gaza Strip is a separated territory of the Palestinians. Israel taxes the Palestinians and these taxes are used for the occupation. Many of the so-called Israeli settlements are on Palestinian land. Often, if an Israeli sets up a shack or an outpost, it is then protected by a wall and becomes a settlement. The Palestinians who used to live on that land lose their home. Often Palestinians are not allowed in the Israeli settlement area so once the wall goes up, Palestinians are separated from friends and family on the other side. If Palestinians want to repair their roofs, they cannot get a permit for the work; if they don't get the permit they are fined and if they get the permit, their home is taken from them or demolished. It is a living sentiment of "damned if you do and damned if you don't."

During her trip to the West Bank, Mary was eager to see Bethlehem. Thinking of it as a holy place of peace, she was shocked into the reality of what some would call "the security state" and others would call overt racism. About one mile outside the city, she was greeted by armed guards, barbed wire, and gun turrets. Palestinians are not allowed to drive a car into the city and must walk the last mile after going through multiple checkpoints where they are questioned over and over: Where are you going? Why are you going there? There are multiple metal detectors. Americans with a blue passport are allowed in, while some visitors, mostly Palestinians, are simply told they cannot enter. The livelihood of many of the residents in Bethlehem has been altered by this level of security. They now make their living touring and driving the tourists who are able to pass this maze of checkpoints.

After the mile-long walk to the city, Mary and her team were guided by an old gentleman who drove them around the city. He took them to Shepherds Field where they saw an olive tree, standing solid against the sky, that was older than the time of Jesus. She thought of all the history that tree had seen. She saw the huge field and could imagine the night sky, and the sheep, and the shepherds, as celebrated in holiday songs. But going through that view was a large wall, an apartheid wall to keep the Palestinians out. *"That is a sin,"* Mary said to the driver. He didn't know what the word "sin" meant. He had originally been an artist but for now, he just kept driving.

"Resilient" is a word Mary would use to describe the Palestinian people she met on the trip. She describes the beautiful glass art made by the Palestinians in Hebron, and the value she places on a small piece she brought back from the region as a memento of her time there. Her eyes look downward as she describes the place of Hebron.

*It is a walled city, by far the most depressing place I have ever been in my whole life. There is a hot wet blanket of anger, sadness and depression there. It is heavy and hard. They live in poverty. The streets have fishnet over them because the settlers throw garbage down onto the children in the streets. Sometimes, the Israeli settlers urinate on the Palestinians below. They used to have a big open market but the Israelis put a sniper tower there and shoot people at random, saying they are a suspected terrorist. There is very little way to make a living. There is poverty and it feels like an open-air prison.* (3)

The Meta Peace Team, with Mary Hanna, Kim Redigan, and a woman named Twila, was staying at a Hebron apartment that was sponsored by the International Solidarity Movement. Known as Al-Kahlil in Hebrew, the 700-year-old city of Hebron is often considered a microcosm of the conflict between the Israelis and the Palestinians. Settlers come to the area because it is financially feasible, and the tribal attitudes of the most zealous fundamentalists among them make life difficult for the Palestinians and their children. The Christian Peacemaker Team (CPT) has a regular presence in the area, working daily to walk Palestinian children to school in Protective Accompaniment. The Meta Peace Team members were working with CPT and the International Solidarity Movement in their mission.

Hebron is surrounded by walls, and there are rows of stalls for food vendors. Beyond the stalls, one steps up onto a ledge leading to a long open-air hallway, with many doors on either side. The doors are steel, with three metal shives locking it to the casing; one above, one on the side and one on the bottom of the door. Bathrooms are a trench that runs into the street. One of these apartments was where the MPT group could stay. The ISM representative who typically stayed there was out of town with business in Jerusalem, so Mary, Kim and Twila were alone in the apartment for the night. Entering through the solid steel door, the apartment opened into a courtyard, which led to a cave-like area where provisions of water and food were held. Beyond that area was the same kind of steel door leading to a room where they would sleep. There were mats on the floor, some books and maps and small lanterns.

It was about 2 a.m. while everyone was sleeping when suddenly there was loud banging on the outer door. Startled awake, Mary and Kim could hear ferocious barking of dogs and people throwing themselves against the door. They could hear tools scraping the steel door, perhaps a wrench to get the door open. Recalling the practice by the Israelis of taking Palestinian property with little to no recourse, the women wondered if the absence of the ISM member from the apartment caused the effort to confiscate the home. Perhaps they didn't realize MPT was staying there, and what would the intruders do if they actually got in and found them there? The women had no cell service to make a phone call, and no address to tell anyone of their whereabouts if they had a phone in the first place. They had no way to reach out to their friends with Christian Peacemaker Team who had a house just blocks away. They were trapped.

Twila remained "asleep" as she tried to cope with the threat. There was no way out. So, Mary and Kim remained huddled together, whispering to each other, trying to develop a plan. They could not do anything until the door was breached. If the intruders were able to get in, the peace team could potentially welcome them, saying *"oh, we thought you were the military, come in and have some water."* Given all the tools for Active Nonviolence they had learned, the only thing they could do was trust, pray and wait. The action at the steel door got quiet for a while, but they returned with more tools, more banging and still the barking of the dogs. Mary and Kim waited, and listened with every molecule in their body. They had to wait until they had something to work with, something to react to. Kim concentrated on centering herself. Mary recalled the wisdom of a friend who once told her, *"When there is nothing to do, do nothing."*

Mary said:

*This was the scariest thing I had ever gone through. I had no tools, there was nothing I could do until they got through those doors. If they were trying to scare us, they were doing a good job. I don't recall feeling fatalistic or panicky. I remember thinking, I just have to wait longer. We were ready to do something, but we didn't know what we needed to do yet.* (4)

So they waited.

Just as the sun started coming up around 6 in the morning, the banging stopped and the hall outside was silent. The peace team stayed in the apartment and did not venture out until the ISM representative returned to the apartment, saying: "What the hell happened to the door!?" The steel door was pocked with dents and spray painted. Once they were finally able to leave the apartment, Kim recalls the lasting message of the experience when she heard the neighbor say to them:

*Oh. Those were just settlers. Welcome to our world. This is what we deal with all the time.* (5)

It became painfully obvious to her that Palestinians experienced terrorism on a regular basis.

*We witnessed the reality of occupation firsthand. This story really isn't about us, but rather about the Palestinians and the terror and fear they live with every day.* (6)

As a peace team, it isn't always about being on the front line or intervening at a demonstration. A great deal of the work is about being a witness and telling the stories. Knowing and sharing these stories can help us see and hear our own government in a much different tone. Kim reflects on her time in Palestine:

*We need to go home and tell our stories, tell their stories and talk with our brothers and sisters to effect change in America. It is easy to be in tear gas, but much harder to talk to each other back home and effect change here.* (7)

Having seen the best and the worst of humanity, Kim says her experience in that region was a turning point in her life. Her first trip to the region was in April 2004 with a peace delegation of forty anti-nuclear, non-proliferative activists. Mordechai Vanunu was to be released from prison and protesters on both sides of the issue were present for the event. Vanunu worked as a nuclear technician for the Israeli nuclear weapons infrastructure, despite Israel's denial of that program. He blew the whistle on the program to the British press in 1986. He had been abducted by Israeli intelligence agents, tried behind closed doors and imprisoned for eighteen years, with eleven of those years in solitary confinement. Anti-nuclear activists wanted to be present when he was freed, in support of his whistle-blowing actions. There were also vociferous right-winged Israeli settlers carrying black roses, calling Vanunu a traitor and throwing eggs at the anti-nuclear supporters. It was a heated environment and many experienced peacekeepers showed up.

Kim recalls that in the midst of all the yelling and tension:

*There was an old man carrying an Israeli flag. I saw a sadness in him as he was walking back and forth with his flag. He wasn't yelling, he was just quietly carrying his flag back and forth. I reached across the barricade between us and handed him some water, saying 'It's really hot today and you look really thirsty. Would you like some water?' He took the water. About fifteen minutes later, he came back to me at the barricade and said to me, 'Do you know the story of Moses in the desert?' I replied, yes. He said, 'You are like Moses. I thought I was going to faint, then you handed me that water.' He took my hand and kissed it. We started talking. He was a Holocaust survivor. We were on two different sides of the barrier, ideologically we were on two different sides of the issue. But it was one of the most profoundly human moments of my life. Nothing was reconciled between us politically, but it was an intense human moment. There would be some who would say to not cross the barrier, but that is not the point. It changed me, and I would like to believe it changed him. Maybe it didn't change our positions, but we cannot go away from that exchange and not see each other as human. We cannot continue to demonize each other.* [8]

━━━━━━━━

One Friday in Bil'in, during a demonstration, Kim noticed a subtle change in the atmosphere, and the people of the village told everyone it was time to back off and retreat. Sometimes internationals keep pushing an issue and unintentionally aggravate a tense situation, but the people who live there know and pay attention to the subtle signs. Kim and her peace team pulled back and retreated with the demonstrators. A short time later, she was sitting on the patio having tea with some of the villagers, interacting with a little girl who was about 4 years old. Kim watched the Israeli soldiers come around the corner and saw a young woman soldier reach into her pocket while they got into formation. She then threw a percussion grenade right into the group. It exploded between the little girl and Kim, splattering her backpack with whatever was in the grenade. Kim's ears were ringing and the little girl was screaming, completely traumatized by the event. It was a random act of terror, man's inhumanity to man. In this case, a woman's inhumanity to women and children.

In Palestine, part of their resistance is their joy. Picture a bride and groom running through tear gas to get to their wedding. People get married, make a home together, have babies, try to do meaningful work and live their lives despite the challenges in their station. They celebrate life, which goes on despite the efforts of those who want them to end. Their resistance is made by living full lives. There is humor in life, like the time Kim saw a soldier with his gold plate name tag with the name "Sniper" on it. Who would have a name plate like that? One had to laugh. Then there was the time in Bethlehem at one of the checkpoints, when a Palestinian man got out of his car and picked up a rifle dropped by one of the Israeli soldiers. The Palestinian man walked up to the soldier and handed his rifle back to him. It was as if both men had a part to play in a tragic story. Both went on about their day, not seeing the irony in the action.

One time in Palestine, Kim and another peace team member went to the South Hebron hills to be present in solidarity with the Cave Dwellers, who lived there. A Bedouin community, the Cave Dwellers lived simple lives governed by the cycles of nature, taking their sheep out to pasture in the morning and returning at night. On the edge of their land were Israeli settlers who were known to beat the Cave Dwellers, poison their wells, and who, just weeks earlier, had beaten a peace worker. Kim's peace team was to provide Unarmed Civilian Protection for the Cave Dwellers as they went with the sheep to their grazing area.

Kim recalls the resilience of the Cave Dwellers and her feeling of kinship with them. They lived on the periphery of the military zone, and the settlers were repeatedly trying to take their land. Their resistance was going out every day with their animals and tending their sheep. Kim easily assimilated into the group, and at one point the matriarch gave her a bath, becoming the first non-community member ever to be so honored. One day, an injured bird flew into the cave and settled there. Kim took it to symbolize a peace dove, and its arrival indicated that perhaps the plight of the Cave Dwellers was going to change. Everyone was cooing over it. A while later, Kim went outside to relieve herself by a nearby tree, and it occurred to her that the peace dove might have another purpose. Sure enough. The Cave Dwellers also thought the bird was a gift from God, but more for their dinner plans than for peace. Being a guest, Kim was served first. She ate with gusto and thanksgiving for their gracious hospitality.

As part of a peace team, awareness of gender is important. Kim recalls a time in Bil'in when the men were gathering to talk politics and smoke. Kim and the other women on the peace team went with the women of the village. They were given access to stories often overlooked by the media; stories of a mother whose son was arrested and detained, stories of the children in their schools and the mother's concerns over what happens to them while they are separated. There were stories of food access or lack thereof, and how to continue providing for safety and the life needs of their families. Often the focus of any movement is on the patriarchal role of resistance, but there is a feminine version as well.

*The unbearable burden of knowing; once you know you cannot un-know, once you see you cannot un-see, once you hear, you cannot un-hear. That is the biggest take-away for anyone going on a peace team. Once you hear these stories, you have lost your innocence, you cannot unhear these stories.* [9]

To effect change in the dynamics between the Israelis and the Palestinians, we need to tell their stories. Sharing the stories presents the reality of the brokenness and the beauty that is profoundly juxtaposed in the region. There needs to be thoughtful and critical analysis, but the telling of stories is the primary place to begin. We cannot be simple clinicians, rather, we have to get into the messiness of the story and tell it.

Activist Barbara Harvey, a lawyer from the Detroit area, is part of the grassroots organization Jewish Voice for Peace. Having grown in up America, she had bought into every bit of the rhetoric about Palestinians being terrorists. But after coming face to face with Palestinian people during her first visit to the area in 1986, she recognized their innate beauty and generosity.

*I was blown away by how wonderful Palestinian society is, how civilized Palestinian people are, and how horribly we've been lied to about Palestinians as terrorists. What is really going on is Israel deliberately inciting violence by pushing people beyond their ability to keep taking it, so Palestinians' only choice is to politely die, leave, or fight back. If they leave, they leave behind their civilization, which took thousands of years to create. Some become suicide bombers because they feel it is their only recourse. Then Israel can call them terrorists and incite more violence.* [10]

While there, Barbara stayed in the old city of East Jerusalem. She was surrounded by stone buildings with wisteria climbing everywhere, casting a lovely scent into the air. People ride around on donkeys, and it appeared to her as she imagined it would appear 2,000 years ago. She awoke at dawn every day to the sound of cocks crowing, stone cutters starting their work, and the call to prayer. It was a soulful way to begin the morning, putting her at peace with the world around her.

As part of her activism with Jewish Voice for Peace, she tells stories to illustrate what is really happening with the Israeli occupation. She reminds me of the 2005 removal of all Jewish people from the Gaza Strip, whether they wanted to leave or not. The Israeli government heralded the move as humanitarian to illustrate their goodness, but in reality, there were nefarious plans in motion. From December 2008 to January 2009, the Gaza War, also known as Operation Cast Lead was launched. Israel's goal was to stop Palestinian rocket fire into Israel, and the Palestinian Hamas stated the rocket fire was in response to Israeli military action. It became known as Israel's biggest invasion of Gaza, using the area as a testing lab for their military weaponry. The Israeli military rained white phosphorous poison over the densely populated Gaza City essentially poisoning the Palestinian people who remained. Considered a violation of international humanitarian law, the substance burns flesh as long as there is oxygen and could burn skin to the bone. When inhaled, it burns like fire in the lungs. The absence of this story in mainstream American media exasperated Barbara, who found coverage only through online sources such as Amnesty International, Electronic Intifada, and Doctors Without Borders. During this campaign, more than 1,400 Palestinians were killed, including more than 1,000 civilians. Thirteen Israelis were killed, including three civilians. Barbara saw a video of a seasoned physician who had been part of Doctors Without Borders for over thirty years weeping as he described the white phosphorous bombing and its aftermath. He described weapons and injuries he saw that suggested the presence of depleted uranium in the bombs. Other bombs, upon exploding, spewed razor-sharp metal that amputated limbs. If they didn't immediately die, those who survived were expected to die more slowly from eventual uranium poisoning. [11]

*It is coldblooded capitalism at work. Israel creates weapons, tests them, then they have weapons fairs. They call it the 'Lab.' They invite military leaders from all over the world to come and show off their new weapons, describing them as 'field tested' and then they make money off them.* [12]

In response to Operation Cast Lead, many peace groups, namely the International Solidarity Movement, tried to break the blockade of boats that were bringing supplies like medicine, food, books and items of daily living to Gaza. Like many of the roads, the waterway was blocked by the Israeli occupying forces. Huwaida Arraf, *"a brilliant and fearless activist,"* co-founded the effort to break the blockade and bring supplies to Gaza. After a harrowing journey through the Mediterranean Sea, with an Israeli spy boat interrupting their communications, the boat reached shore to the cheers of thousands of Gazans who greeted them, grateful that the larger world had not forgotten them. [12]

For those going to the region as part of a peace team, getting ready for such an international trip is often fraught with multiple emotions; excitement, mixed with fear and caution. Linda Sartor has served on multiple peace teams; in Palestine with the Meta Peace Team and the International Solidarity Movement, in Iraq and Afghanistan with Voices in the Wilderness, and in Sri Lanka with the Nonviolent Peaceforce. The process of getting ready for her first peace team placement to Palestine in 2002 is well captured in her book, *Turning Fear Into Power: How I Confronted the War on Terror.* [13] As she faced her insecurities about her participation on a peace team in such a volatile area, she had to confront her fears head-on.

*I need to distinguish the fears that I really need to honor from those I do not need to allow to alter my path.* [14]

The support of family, friends and those already doing the work of peace teams was instrumental in her ability to get to the region. Particularly helpful was the instruction from a member of the International Solidarity Movement, who said:

*We are not siding with Palestinians against the Israelis, but siding against violence and for a peace based on justice that will allow Israelis and Palestinians to live in mutual security.* [15]

After her arrival at Ben Gurion Airport she took a taxi to Jerusalem. Also along for the taxi ride were two Jewish women from New York who were planning to visit family in the area. Once they learned of Linda's hotel plans, one of the women was appalled and begged Linda to change her plans.

*That's Arab! What do you want to go there for?!? It's like going to Harlem. The friend who told you to stay at that hotel is not a friend!* [16]

Even though Linda is not Jewish, the woman was frightened for her. But the blatant racism was hard to miss.

After meeting up with her peace team, Linda and the others were trained for a couple days in the specific issues of the area and their plans for placement in the region. Their first assignment was in Balata Camp, which is a village of permanent homes for Palestinian refugees. In Linda's words:

*It is late in the day as we get close to Balata. A Palestinian ambulance passes us. Ambulances are the only Palestinian vehicles that are out on the street during curfew. A tank further ahead fires a line of machine gun fire at the ground in front of the ambulance and us — a very scary warning not to proceed further. At first, we are jolted and swerve to the side in unison. Someone reminds us of (our instruction) to 'ground,' and then we turn to walk the other direction.*

*The ambulance stops and we all climb aboard. The two Palestinians in the vehicle are grim as they drive us around to another entrance into Balata Camp. It is growing dark and we know that it is dangerous to be out after dark because soldiers can't see who we are. We see that we have to walk past another tank. The eleven of us clump closely together and put our hands up as we pass. I keep reassuring myself with the idea that it would be bad public relations for an Israeli soldier to hurt a U.S. citizen since their operations would not be possible without our funding."* [17]

Linda worked with experienced peacekeepers in the region who know the languages of Hebrew, Arabic, and English. In Balata Camp, the Israeli soldiers had arrived in the area a few days before and were going from home to home, bashing through walls from neighboring house to neighboring house. The families were begging the soldiers to use their doors, and allow them to move their belongings to help minimize the damage. The team eventually learned the soldiers were breaking through walls inside the homes to make a passage-way, so Israeli soldiers did not have to walk through the streets where they felt vulnerable to sniper bullets. But the only people with guns were the Israeli soldiers. After bashing the door-sized holes through the common walls between two homes, the soldiers spray painted large arrows on walls to direct the soldiers through rooms to the makeshift doorways. This is terror for the women and children in the homes. The men of the camp were taken and held captive in a nearby mosque, some of them beaten and deprived of food and water for hours and days.

Sleep was challenging for Linda despite the fatigue of travel. Even with the extensive training, the work of the peace team was challenging and difficult, with her immediate placement into the Balata Camp, where occupying soldiers conducted daily raids into homes "looking for something." Days were spent with the affected families to provide solidarity and accompaniment. Often, injured Palestinians were escorted to the clinics, with notes to present to the drivers of the tanks in order to be allowed passage. Throughout the day peace teams accompany Palestinians as they move through the streets for any reason, for if they were unaccompanied, there would be potential for beatings or other forms of violence.

One day, Linda and her team partner, Star, were escorting three men to the mosque when Israeli soldiers stopped them and took the men's IDs. The men were instructed to stand against a wall with their hands on the bricks. Gradually, other men were brought to the wall in the same manner, with the soldiers speaking in Hebrew throwing humiliating epithets at the Palestinian men. Linda found herself stationed between the men and the soldiers and she did not move from her interruptive position. Star stayed off to the side, but Linda stayed in her position near the men. Suddenly, her phone rang and there was a radio announcer from America who called to get an update on her story. Linda started relating the events of that exact moment, standing among about thirty-five Israeli soldiers who had about twenty Palestinian men lined up against a wall. She tried to stay on the phone as long as possible, realizing the whole radio listening audience was witness to the actions of these soldiers. Eventually, Linda hung up the phone and was approached by an Israeli soldier who told her to go home. Linda responded, *"No."* The exasperated soldier was not sure what to do with her, so simply walked away.

Star signaled to Linda to leave the area, thinking the energy had shifted and the soldiers were feeling antagonized. Just then, the soldiers instructed the Palestinian men to move along on the road toward the mosque. Linda and Star left the area and returned to the family with whom they were staying. The fate of the men escorted by the soldiers was not known to Linda, but for the tense time she spent at the wall, she felt her presence had made a difference. [18]

Later that night, while talking with fellow peace team members about their future plans, news spread through the camp that the soldiers had left. They went out onto the street.

*… a number of people have gathered, all expressing a huge sense of relief. I notice one woman busily sweeping up the mess the soldiers left behind. The Palestinians seem to have adjusted to this life with soldiers coming, committing various abuses, and then leaving. The Palestinians seem accustomed to cleaning up the messes of the soldiers repeatedly, erasing the evidence of their presence as soon as they leave and bouncing back to lives of normalcy as much as possible. I feel sad and somewhat ashamed that these destructive disruptions are such a common occurrence.* [19]

Linda's most recent trip to Palestine was in June 2018 with the Meta Peace Team. There were four people on the team, including Elliott Adams, John and Laurie from Vermont, and Linda. They trained as a group in Detroit for five days, getting to know each other's strengths and challenges in order to be ready to work with each other once on the ground. Having participated in other peace organizations, Linda found this type of training with the assigned peace team very effective. Once settled in the region, the peace team was housed at various places, including homes and schools, on office floors, or in tents. They slept on mats on the floor, with a pillow and a sheet. There was a daily diet of hummus, pita bread, chicken and vegetables. Sometimes they stayed at a place with a kitchen and made their own dinners, but most often they were guests in a home or ate what the vendors offered on the street. Any free time was spent writing reports and journaling the details of the day, which helped foster their reflections once they returned home.

The Meta Peace Team usually works collaboratively with other peace teams in the area. One evening on a city street in Palestine, International Solidarity Movement members had left for the day and members of MPT were planning their next day. Suddenly, one of the shopkeepers on the street yelled, *"Soldiers!"* and the other townspeople ran into their homes and shops for protection. The MPT members stood alone in the street wearing their bright yellow Peace Team vests. They stayed in their position and did not scatter. Eventually they were approached by a soldier who told them it was dangerous for them to be there and to leave. The soldiers took pictures of their passports, which can sometimes lead to blacklisting, making it difficult to return to the region. But nothing came of the action. Gratefully, there was no other altercation. Linda notes:

*Often, being on a peace team involves a lot of time just being, rather than doing. Our being present changes the behavior of the Israeli soldiers and the settlers and often prevents violence. Our presence interrupts their 'business as usual.' This, our presence, is our intervention.* [20]

Reflecting on her experiences in Palestine, Linda states:

*It isn't about getting rid of fear. It is having a different relation-*

*ship with fear. Our presence changes the dynamics and opens up the space for other local peacemakers to do their work. We accompany them, but they are doing their work.* [21]

Upon returning from an area of perpetual conflict, many peace team members find it helpful to process their experiences with each other and sometimes with a counselor skilled in working with the stress of trauma. Putting these experiences into words, whether written or spoken, helps give meaning to the experience. Meta Peace Team members give presentations, write articles, speak to students, politicians and leaders in education and government. Only by educating our fellow citizens and our lawmakers can better policies be developed to end the Israeli occupation and support both the Palestinians and the Israelis in their quest for a homeland and the potential for unification. As on-the-ground witnesses, peace team members hope that lasting change can be made in policy affecting the entire region. In her book, Linda writes:

*Through telling my story, I hope to inspire readers to get more in touch with their own inner wisdom and to follow their hearts' longings even when it is scary. My belief is that our fears keep us small and prevent us from actualizing our full contributions, and that the powers of domination in our world create and perpetuate cultures of fear in order to stay in control. I hope that the more we all learn to accept fear and follow our hearts anyway (no matter how big or small are the tasks we are called to do), the more likely we as a global society will find our way out of the bad times in which we find ourselves now.* [22]

We may not have any control over violence, but our actions can get in the way of violence. Sometimes our getting in the way is direct and often it is indirect. But there *is* something we can do. Telling the stories from witnesses on the ground is a start.

*An immigrant and her child seeking legal asylum at the U.S./Mexico border*

## CHAPTER EIGHT

# AT THE BORDER

*We are in such a climate of hate right now. We're seeing diminishing acts of kindness and love because fear of the stranger has been so deeply cultivated in us. Breaking down that us-and-them binary is part of the work of love. We need to challenge all of the binaries we face and try to see where to find a relationship with the 'other' — the one we fear — so that we can enact compassion.*
—Sharon Salzberg

It was unseasonably cold with overnight temperatures around 30 degrees Fahrenheit and daytime temperatures struggling to reach 40 degrees. They stayed in a rental house in Tijuana that, although spacious, had no heat. Still, the team of six women trudged on, doing the work of a peace team at the U.S./Mexico border. Rather than months of preparation typical for an international team, this team had been put together over five weeks; organizing air flights, arranging housing, transportation once on the ground, setting up trainings, and fundraising to pay for it all. The team consisted of Mary Hanna, Kathleen Hernandez, Kim Redigan, Linda Sartor, Amy Schneidhorst and Pat Thornburg. This ten-day trip started in mid-February 2019, and the team returned home near the end of the month filled with stories, emotions, and reflections on what they witnessed at the border.

A few months earlier, Elliott Adams and Kathleen Hernandez had gone to the border between San Diego and Tijuana to assess the possibility of fielding a peace team to the area; making connections with other peace teams and human rights organizations; evaluating logistics of getting there and staying there; and determining where the skills of a peace team would be most utilized. It was determined the time was ripe for a peace team, in fact there was a sense of urgency, given the emotionally charged rhetoric of whether to build a wall at the border and the growing number of people seeking legal asylum. Thousands of people were trying to escape violent civil unrest in countries south of Mexico, countries ravaged by right-wing vigilantes and organized gangs.

Coming from various states across America, team members arrived in San Diego and spent the evening organizing their itinerary for the trip. On their first full day, they held a Meta Peace Team Nonviolence Skills Training for more than thirty people at the San Diego Peace Center. People interested in learning the skills of nonviolence and potentially serving on peace teams at the border participated, practicing the role plays of potential interactions where these skills could be utilized. Later that night, the team crossed the border. The six women could not fit in the vehicle with all the luggage at the same time, so three went on foot through the border crossing.

Expecting a long wait with a careful examination of their luggage and the purpose of their trip, the passengers were surprised to be waved through the checkpoint. No one ever looked at their passports or gave them a stamp signaling their presence in the country. Those on foot easily walked through the checkpoint as well.

Housing had been arranged by Kathleen, who lives in San Diego and had been actively engaged with numerous human rights organizations at the border. She had many contacts in the area, which is vital for any international peace team. The peace team stayed at a rental house in Tijuana, which had six beds. It was a large house, perhaps in its heyday had been a grand place to entertain guests. But now it was sparsely furnished, had few supplies, and it was without heat. It was surrounded by a tall fence, with a padlocked gate. Barbed wire ran along the top of the fence surrounding the property. The team later learned Tijuana is the fifth most dangerous city in the world, so security was an issue.

The Meta Peace Team had been invited to Tijuana by Al Otro Lado, which is a bi-national, direct legal services organization serving indigent deportees, migrants, and refugees. Al Otro Lado means "to the other side." Starting as a project in 2012, Al Otro Lado's organization and services greatly increased in the fall of 2018 as so-called "caravans" made their way to the U.S./Mexico border. Their services include a daily "*charla*," or chat about the process of legal immigration and asylum-seeking. Also provided are consultations with immigration lawyers, free medical care, and group daycare for the children while parents seek counsel. Simple food is available, and people can register and make copies of documents. All of this work is done by volunteers, some offer their help for a few days, some stay for months or as long as they can. The orientation includes education about each service area, along with information about Tijuana and how to safely navigate the region. At the end of each day, time is set aside for the volunteers to share a joy and a heartbreak experienced that day. Given the nature of the work, there would be things witnessed that could cause tears, which ultimately would not serve the people whose lives are already filled with chaos and uncertainty. If the emotional strain is too much, then volunteers are encouraged to tap out and take a break. Crayons, Play-Doh and exercise were available for those needing an emotional outlet.

The first day included an orientation at Al Otro Lado, and by

6:45 a.m. the next day, the peace team was at El Chaparral, the area at the border in Tijuana where people gather seeking legal asylum. They hit the ground running.

Every day taxis and buses deliver people to the area, and many people arrive on foot from across the city. They come from Haiti, Cameroon, Honduras, Russia, Turkey, El Salvador, Venezuela, Guatemala and other countries in South America. Multiple languages are spoken in the area, including English, Spanish, Creole, French, and Russian, along with many other dialects from smaller regions across the world. Off to the side are four-foot tall letters spelling "Tijuana," brightly colored with the names of the counties in the area, as if it were a tourist attraction. At the pedestrian entrance to the border, there is a tent under which sits a card table. Two asylum seekers stand at the table with a frayed composition notebook, taking names of those waiting in line. They hand each person a tiny piece of paper no bigger than a paper pulled from a fortune cookie, upon which they write a four-digit number. They are told to hold onto this paper until their number is called, which can typically take four to six weeks. If they don't have the paper when their number is called, they have to start the process over again. Once the people working this table note their own number is called, then two new asylum seekers step forward to carry on this work with the notebook and the tiny papers.

The area is patrolled by Groupa Beta, which is the self-described humanitarian wing of the Mexican National Institute of Migration, charged with controlling the flow of legal asylum seekers into the U.S. The U.S. Customs and Border Patrol (CBP) delegates the management of "la lista," or the list, to Beta. Each day, the CBP contacts Beta with the number of asylum seekers who can start processing that day, which averages between five and forty people a day. The "list," which is a process called "metering," is somewhat arbitrary as some people can advance to the head of the line without the typical wait.

Each day, Beta makes the announcement to the anxiously await-ing people, calling out the numbers chosen for the day, and then the scramble begins. While preparing to board the bus, all belong-ings have to be left behind as each person is allowed only the cloth-ing closest to their skin and their documents. The blankets, the pictures, the soap, the water bottles, the backpacks, the dolls, the food, the toothbrushes, the medications, the coats, the Bibles, their shoelaces and anything other than the clothes on their back is left behind. Mothers, fathers, grandmothers and grandfathers scurry to write with permanent marker on the forearms of the children their names and contact information, having been told they will be separated from their children and the chances of reunification are greater if they do so. Children younger than 3 are usually allowed to stay with the parents. Otherwise, separation in inevitable.

---

One cold morning, Kim and Kathleen were working as human rights observers witnessing the registration process at El Chapar-ral. People stood waiting to register or to hear their number called. Kathleen recalled seeing a little girl about 6 or 7 years old standing with her mom and younger sister. The girl was shivering and obvi-ously cold, although she wore a light jacket. Unable to personally interact with the people in her role as observer, Kathleen struggled with how to help this child. Wearing a coat herself, she instructed Kim to raise her hood over her head while she held the gaze of the little girl. Speaking only with her eyes and pointing to her hood, Kathleen watched as the little girl copied the action, placing her own hood and tying it around her chin. It was a small act of kind-ness that took only minutes, but the feeling of love and connection to this little girl is seared in Kathleen's memory. [1]

Handing out fliers with information guiding people to Al Otro Lado, Pat Thornburg met a man from Honduras. She started chat-

ting with him about the weather, his health, and the services of Al
Otro Lado. When she told him about how many nice people she
had met in Honduras on her travels, the man's face became fearful and dark, as if washed with memories of traumatic times. Pat
recalled feeling there was nothing about this process of immigration, inhumane as it could be, that could match his previous experience and his psychological pain. Another person she met in line
at El Chaparral was a Muslim man seeking asylum from Turkey.
Pat said the man appeared to be around 30 years old and sturdy
enough to endure the hardships ahead in the asylum process. He
buoyantly stated, *"It's going to be so much better in America!"* [2] The
sense of hopefulness was palpable in so many faces at the border.
They are not the first to feel a sense of devotion to America and
a longing for a better future. Our history is rich in stories of pil-
grims, indentured servants, immigrants and refugees traveling to
America, enduring challenging journeys, hunger, and separation
from their homeland.

After their numbers are called, the chosen ones gather at the
border for their next step. One morning, Beta noted there was
room for *"one more person!"* People rushed to the officers, but
most belonged to families of at least two or three people who were
not willing to separate at this stage of the process. Finally, a tall
black man raised his hand and said, *"I'll go."* He was an activist
from Haiti and had been in Tijuana with his family for a while,
continuing his activist work in that area while preparing for their
immigration. He hugged and kissed his children, embraced his
wife and said goodbye. It was heartbreaking to see this family split
up, but the look of hope on his face was evident. It was a moment
of deep intimacy for this family, causing many to look away with
tears stinging their eyes, trying to allow this family some privacy
in their parting. [3]

Collecting themselves after the emotional calling of numbers,
members of the Meta Peace Team went to work, handing out per-

manent markers, making sure people had their warmest piece of clothing possible closest to their skin, and distributing donated clothing for those without a safe option. Each person whose number was called was also given a Mylar blanket, similar to the type of foil blanket given to marathon runners at the end of a race. After months of waiting, the asylum seekers board the bus and are driven into the United States. The bus is driven about one mile, then loops back to the exact other side of the border and empties the people into the underground bunkers to await further processing.

The bunker is made of concrete, with rooms about twelve feet by eight feet. There is a metal door. There are no windows. There is one toilet set aside with four-foot walls surrounding it. There is sometimes a table in the room, otherwise there is no furniture. There is no heat in these rooms and the facility is often referred to as the *hielera* or "icebox." Like foil-wrapped baked potatoes in a pan, people huddle together wrapped in their Mylar blankets, trying to stay warm. Family members are often separated at this time and stay in these rooms until called for further processing, which can take a couple of weeks.

Further processing includes a "credible fear" interview. If CBP authorities at the border believe an asylum seeker has enough proof that his or her life is in danger, the asylum seeker is allowed to continue the process. If the "credible fear" interview does not convince the authorities at the time of their meeting, then the people are sent back to Tijuana. Sometimes family members are separated if the risk does not entail the entire family. Once it is determined there is "credible risk," the asylum seekers are fitted with a tracking cuff on their ankles, similar to those used for prisoners on parole. They are allowed to stay in the United States with a sponsor and await further court hearings, but at any time they may still be deported. While they wait, they are not allowed to seek employment and must pay for the tracking cuff on their ankle.

United States and international law notes the overarching goal of the modern refugee regime is to provide protection to individuals forced to flee their homes because their countries are unwilling or unable to protect them. They are to be allowed into the country, where processing can then occur. The legality of refusing people at the border or sending them back if they "fail" the interview is highly questionable, with many legal authorities labeling it fully illegal. Many of the countries from which the asylum seekers flee have been ravaged by war, debilitated by sanctions, or devastated by natural disasters. The foreign policies of many countries, including the United States have created or allowed these countries to slip into utter chaos, resulting in repressive and violent military regimes, gangs and organized crime, which creates a clear threat to the lives of their citizens. It is no small decision to leave their homeland, risking life and limb as they attempt to seek protection in other countries, often ending at the border of the United States. Countries around the world are struggling with the delicate balancing act of allowing asylum seekers a safe refuge while not overwhelming the use of resources in the host country. But rather than focusing on the problems in the countries of origin, the U.S. and many countries around the world take a reactionary approach. It is like spitting on a fire rather than addressing the cause.

Our perspective of the immigration process and its causes is too often very narrow. Some have been led to believe that people seeking asylum are criminals, drug dealers, and rapists. Another view focuses on those trying to enter the country under false pretense, claiming imminent threats or claiming family status with someone else's children. Some people believe that immigrants take jobs and resources away from Americans. Others see immigrants as adding a rich cultural diversity to America, by role modeling dedication to work, family cohesion, and the commitment to a better life. Another point of view focuses on the pain in the human family, and it is the role of the most privileged among us to care for the most vulnerable among us. Whatever the perspective, it is through these lenses that today's immigrants are seen. As with any large number of people, there will be as many different stories as there are people. To make assumptions about the whole, given the actions of a few, is one of the major failings of humans across the globe.

Volunteers from all over the world are trying to humanely address the challenges facing asylum seekers and the increase in immigration. Usually, violence in their homeland causes them to flee, but they are met with a different form of harm at the border of the U.S. Those working at the border are trying to stop the cycle of violence. Peace team members are challenged to remain politically neutral and focus on the work of supporting a humane process for legal asylum.

The Meta Peace Team volunteers stayed busy at El Chaparral every morning, handing out fliers with directions to Al Otro Lado, where asylum seekers could get advice and information about the immigration process. By the time the bus pulled away loaded with those whose numbers were called that day, the area clears and people return to their shelters or to another homeless night on the streets of Tijuana. The card table and tent are put away until the next day. The peace team then moves to volunteer at Al Otro Lado. An impressive and efficient organization funded by donations, Al Otro Lado is a place where the best of humanity tries to help those who are fleeing the worst of humanity.

Each day, asylum seekers line up at Al Otro Lado to be registered. They give their names, their countries of origin, and the number of people in their families. Documents are copied and returned. Assessments are made along the line to determine their needs so as to best direct them to the services available. Kathleen, being fluent in Spanish, worked at the registration computer taking information from each person. Pat, having a working understanding of Spanish and experience as a pediatric nurse, was able to assess people while in line. Anyone needing medical attention was escorted to the area in the building set aside for such care. Medical care is available for anyone in the area, not just the asylum seekers. While MPT was there, the medical team consisted of volunteers from Alaska. Other than a few cases of lice or scabies, most people needed medical care because of nagging coughs. Overall, people were relatively hearty. Those who were infirmed knew not to attempt the journey in the first place or were left behind.

At Al Otro Lado, Pat met a young woman who had just given birth to her second child the day before. The mother beamed at the sleeping six-pound infant, while her 3-year-old son clung to his dad's leg. They were so happy and so proud of their family, eagerly showing the workers their newest member. Pat recalled their joy and their hope, and her own dread for what they faced. The baby would be safe, staying with the mom, with skin-to-skin potentially keeping the baby's temperature stable while they wait in the *hielera*. But she worried about the 3-year-old, who would most likely be separated from his parents.

Recalling her days as a pediatric nurse, she shuddered with the memory of having to tell parents their child was alive but that the road ahead would be fraught with tough times.

*The separation of families, especially children from parents, risks serious reactive attachment disorders and post-traumatic stress disorders. It was a heartbreaking situation to witness.* [4]

The beauty of humanity in the face of such uncertainty came through in many ways. Kathleen recalls an incident that happened on one cool afternoon, while people waited at the border. The husband of an attorney at Al Otro Lado brought 200 rolled tacos, and set up containers filled with avocado sauce, fresh cut cucumbers, chopped cilantro, pickled radishes and napkins.

*Families lined up, so calm and so grateful. There was no push-*

*ing, no shoving, just people patiently waiting. Everyone got two tacos, no matter how old or how young. I've never done something where my hand took something so valuable and placed it into someone else's hand. It was so needed and so appreciated. Some of these people had just arrived. They took their tacos and sat on the ground like a picnic. This simple gesture of humanity brought tears to my eyes.* [5]

While volunteering with Al Otro Lado, some peace team members worked security detail at the "door." Given the risks of gang members or organized crime members trying to thwart people's efforts at fleeing, security at the door is a vital issue. Educating people of their rights takes a bite out of organized crime and every effort is made to keep an eye out for those who are stalking the asylum seekers. Al Otro Lado gets regular death threats, so MPT was always on the lookout at the door. Everyone in the building must wear a nametag at all times and leave it there at the end of the day to be counted. Those waiting in line at the door are assessed for their needs and their wrists are stamped accordingly with the daily theme: a green monkey, a purple frog, an orange bird, etc. Each day it is a different color and a different animal. One stamp clears a person to go to the third floor accompanied by a volunteer for the *charla*, for food, or for daycare. Two stamps clear a person to be accompanied to medical care. Much of the day was spent "running" people up and down the stairs to their various destinations for services. The *charla* started at 2 p.m. each day, so no one was allowed to enter the building after that time unless a meal or medical care was needed. Throughout the day, anyone entering the building was accompanied by a volunteer, and the MPT peace team assisted in this role.

While assessing people in line, Kim was deeply affected by an El Salvadoran man holding the hand of his 10-year-old son. Kim had been to El Salvador four times in the past with her high school students, and knew the challenges in the country. During their civil war in the 1980s, many Salvadorans fled to Los Angeles, and they witnessed the infiltration of gangs in the city. Many joined in self-defense while in America. Once they were able to return to their country, and often they were forced to return, the practices of the gang culture were taken back with them. El Salvador was still plagued by violence, as gang culture became an American export. Currently, gangs remain a violent threat to many families, and when boys reach a certain age, they are expected to join. If not, they can be killed and their families threatened. Dressed formally and standing proudly yet quietly, this man held tight to the hand of his son, trying to the best of his ability to protect him from the gangs by seeking asylum in America. Kim could only imagine the love of this father for his son, that he would risk everything to keep him safe from the gangs. [6]

Mary Hanna tells a story about three teenage boys who were trying to escape the gang threat in Nicaragua. The oldest was 18 years old, his brother and another boy were both 16. The plight of their parents was unclear. Now beyond the gangs, their biggest fear was separation at the border, given the minor status of the two 16-year-olds. Speaking with fear in their eyes, they wanted to stay together throughout the process. They spoke of music, and the glorified idea they had of life in America. But they lowered their eyes while realizing their fate was in the hands of those at the "credible threat" interview, hoping they would hear their desire to avoid dying on the streets in their country. [7]

In line for the *charla* was a mom with her three sons and their grandmother. The boys were about 12, 9 and 3 years old. Kim spent about an hour with the family, talking with the kids and interacting with them while they waited. They were just regular kids practicing their English with Kim, who was practicing her Spanish with them. The oldest eventually ran across the street to buy a piece of jalapeno candy to share with Kim, thanking her for the teachings.

The middle child was quieter, almost shy but listening intently to the lessons. The 3-year-old was completely enamored with airplanes, and every time one was overhead, he would point to the sky and exclaim in Spanish, *Mira!* "Look!" It was such a picture of humanity. It was as if they were waiting in line to get into the movie theater for their favorite show, but the look of uncertainty and fear in the mother's eyes brought the gravity of the situation back to reality. [8]

It was a heartbreaking realization to see the 4- and 5-year-old girls with their pink coats and child-sized backpacks waiting with their parents, or the little boys playing with a straw they found on the ground. They exuded such a sense of trust and innocence. But those around them knew what lay ahead and felt a sense of dread over the sheer gamble these families were taking. Mary reflects:

*It was hard to see the little kids coming up who were so cute and so trusting. They were happy because they had two green monkey stamps on their wrists. They are happy because they are going to a new place to live, or so they have been told. But we know that when their number is called, it is going to be utter chaos. They will be separated from their parents, they will be staying in freezing cold conditions, and who knows when they will be reunited with their family. It made me want to cry. This is torture for these people. But we didn't want to crush their hope.* [9]

MPT peace team member Amy Schneidhorst spent much of her days as a lookout on security detail at the door, and she commented on the "ordinariness" of watching the comings and goings of people who could be either asylum seekers or tourists. She had to reconcile the difference of what she saw at the border with her preconceptions of what she thought a refugee should look like, what she'd been taught in her childhood.

*It was like watching a movie without the soundtrack, but there was a deep sense of foreboding realizing what was at stake for many of the people milling around.* (10)

She could recall trips she had taken in the past, and inevitably she would hear stories of fellow travelers befallen with some event where they needed to trust someone for help. And someone would always come forward.

*It occurred to me, that MPT and the people at Al Otro Lado played that role. We weren't going to exploit them, prey on them, or hurt them. We were trustworthy. We were just there trying to direct them to the help they needed, for the support they needed in the process.* (11)

According to Kim, the real heroes of the day are the organizers of Al Otro Lado, who show up every day working for the humane treatment and processing of people seeking legal asylum at the U.S./Mexico border. At the end of each day, there is a debriefing time for all the volunteers who served that day. There are usually about forty people from all over the world who come to do this work in the various service fields offered at Al Otro Lado. The typical trends of the day are discussed, countries most represented with asylum seekers are tracked, and the numbers getting through for further processing are announced.

Mary admits to being brought to tears during the daily debriefing.

*They were tears of appreciation at the end of the day sitting in the room with all these people from around the world, donating their time day in and day out, to be the face of compassion for the United States. To be that neighbor as we have all been taught to 'Love thy neighbor.' To stand out in the cold and rain every day, at the crack of dawn and work until nightfall. One guy in his free time said he would teach people Creole, because he was getting so many people from Haiti. These were people who celebrated the smallest things, like when a kitten was born. They use their own money to get there and stay there to do this work. Al Otro Lado works hard and they show appreciation for everyone who comes to help.* (12)

---

The work of the Meta Peace Team was not done after their debriefing with Al Otro Lado. Typically, after grabbing a quick dinner in the area, MPT worked with other groups doing humanitarian work. A group called Border Angels adheres to the words of Jesus when he said, *"When I was hungry you gave me something to eat. I was thirsty and you gave me something to drink, I was a stranger and you invited me in."* (13) They place water supplies throughout the desert, provide resources at border rescue stations, and have a day-laborer outreach program. The peace team worked with the Border Angels doing human rights monitoring at the border crossings where people attempt to walk across illegally. It was often pouring rain and cold, but they could endure the conditions and discomfort as temporary, realizing asylum seekers live with these conditions every day. Many asylum seekers took advantage of the shelters provided by the churches in the area, but many others lived under tents or cardboard boxes as they waited for their number to be called.

Near the end of their trip, MPT partnered with the Unified U.S. Deported Veterans group. Often these men were brought to the U.S. as children. As U.S. veterans who served in places such as Afghanistan and Iraq, they, like many on active duty in the military, often suffered from PTSD. If the veteran's PTSD led to alcohol or drug abuse, they sometimes wound up in the penal system. Their record would be enough to have them deported "back" to a country they did not know. Often they did not even speak the language because they had not been raised there.

The group is struggling to fight for their veteran rights and benefits. MPT attended their event called, "Thank You for Your Service, Now Get Out of My Country." It showcased the personal stories of the veterans affected by this deportation practice. One man noted that his mother had filed his birth certificate incorrectly. He got into the military with this birth certificate, but once home from the service, the mistake was exposed and he was deported. One vet recalled completing his paperwork for citizenship but being on active duty in Afghanistan, he was unable to attend his scheduled hearing and was deported upon return from duty. A man named Hector noted that once he dies, his body could return to America to be buried in Arlington and his wife will get an American flag, but while alive he is not allowed to return. There are many attempts at legislation granting citizenship to those immigrants who have served in the U.S. military, but in the meantime, their wait for justice continues.

The next day, there was a march including the Unified U.S. Deported Veterans, the Muslim Latinex group and the Municipal Police Youth Group. Their mission was to pick up trash from the grounds around Tijuana on the march route, and they invited MPT to field a peace team during the march. Wearing their peace team vests, the team of six women walked the route with the participants.

Linda and Kim were an affinity team and along the march route, they came upon a very inebriated man who was screaming things in a stream of consciousness manner and being alarmingly disruptive. Linda and Kim tried to be a buffer between him and the marchers. There was concern that the man would be arrested by the federal police. So Kim and Linda engaged him in conversation, using their nonviolence skills of listening, aligning and distraction. They learned that he was from Memphis, Tennessee. They ascertained that he suffered from some mental illness. And they were able to keep him preoccupied until he could be delivered to his appointment at the dental clinic. (14)

In a celebratory moment after the march, the various groups gathered for photographs. Kathleen was impacted by the image of the military uniformed youth group smiling for the picture, with the peace flags from the U.S. Deported Veterans waving in the background. All through their time at the border, the team witnessed quiet statements of resistance and resilience such as this. The vets have planted gardens of flowers and vegetables near the border. People have painted colorful designs of graffiti on the metal girds of the current walls separating countries and families, beautifully noting "Love Resists." They brought piñatas to the children living at a shelter in a church in the area. (15) There is tragedy and there is joy, as life goes on with weddings, births, and picnics on the lawn. It is easy to feel overwhelmed with the enormity and implications of what is happening for immigrants and asylum seekers across the world.

Pat Thornburg puts it in perspective:

*Every step makes a difference. It is easy to get discouraged, but you know what? The Berlin Wall came down. If we can see this growth, we can change and become humane again. I saw it in the volunteers, in the hope of the people waiting at the border, and I see that hope in my granddaughters. We can learn, we can grow, and we can change.* (16)

After the march, MPT visited with the veterans group while they ate. It was then time to leave Tijuana, and again, some of the team walked across the border while Mary and Kathleen drove the vehicle across. It took forty-five minutes to walk across, unchecked once again. It took the drivers five hours to cross, given the long wait at the checkpoint. According to Mary, there is still no stamp in her passport from this entire trip.

Once home, the members of the team gave presentations to inform and educate their communities about the realities on the ground at the border. Kim implored people to become involved.

*Whatever your job is, you can find a resistance point. It is a moral imperative to challenge these things, and anyone resisting this needs to be supported.* [17]

After battling a bout of bronchitis, Mary was back to work in the office at the Meta Peace Team. There are hopes to create a hub for the Meta Peace Team in San Diego, of holding many more trainings and placing a peace team at the border on a regular basis. There is always the struggle with fundraising to support these actions, although the need for such work is urgent and imperative. It is a perennial challenge to balance the work of activism with the realities of financial funding. But the daily work moves forward. Mary has this view:

*What I saw when I was there was that this is a really big system, it isn't just one person who is creating the system. There are people who are complicit in this system all the way down the line. Only dismantling the system, exposing it then dismantling it will have a long-term effect.* [18]

━━━━━━━━━

As I heard the stories of what is actually happening at the border of our country, I cannot help but think this is not who we are. We are a country of immigrants. We get so busy and wrapped up in our daily living, we allow the stories of our ancestors to yellow with the pages of history. The details of their mythic story and the smell of their sweat in the labor of their journey has faded with time. I think about my own ancestors who came to America during the potato famines in Ireland, many of whom went through Ellis Island. I can imagine that like many immigrants, they settled in the Irish Catholic part of town, and the smell of sausage, corned beef and cabbage filled their streets. Then there was the German part of town, the Italian, the Russian and the Polish parts of town, each with its own smells and its own language, all of it wafting into the air and landing on laundry drying on clothes lines stretched between their buildings. As time went on, these families moved further into America, learned new recipes, new words, new ways. Before they knew it, they identified as American rather than Irish, and it was something special once a year to make corned beef and cabbage.

I wonder about these immigrants seeking asylum now, fleeing a distant land ravaged by famine, hunger, poverty, violence, and war. They come seeking a new land to find the basics for their survival; safety, food, shelter. How different is their journey from the one my ancestors took? Were my ancestors shunned and greeted with closed doors and suspicious eyes peeking through the curtains? Did someone reach out to them to help them learn English, find housing, and meaningful work? I don't know the answers to those questions, and maybe my not knowing the details of their sweat and tears makes it easier to not consider the plight of immigrants today. A part of us has forgotten who we are and how we are connected to each other. Perhaps those who wish to close the door to America have lost their own faith in the American Dream of abundance and growth. Instead, they hang on to a sense of "us" and "them" and an ideology of scarcity. We see diminishing acts of kindness as the flames of fear feed a belief in a separation from those deemed to be "other." It will take many voices to stop the flow of oxygen to this flame, and instead stoke the belief in our shared humanity, where we break down the "us and them binary" and focus on the work of compassion. Where we renew our faith in the American Dream, and realize that our strength comes from the many different stories we bring to this tapestry.

*Dwight Washington listening to a resident of Flint, Michigan, during the water crisis*

## CHAPTER NINE

# EVERYDAY PEOPLE

*The shortest distance between a human being and
the truth is a story. Powerful stories reflect powerful
truths and awaken compassion in the human family.*
—*Cynthia Brix*

As the first-year college students filed into the room, it was easy to see who had been part of the jock and jokester groups in high school. The young men elbowed each other and sauntered to their seats in the back of the circle of chairs. This Bystander Intervention Training was part of their curriculum for the day, and I began introducing the value and application of tactics to de-escalate violence. The jokester group started making comments in the back of the room. Leaning toward his buddy, one of the young men laughingly said, *"Like maybe in domestic violence, it's okay to hit them with an open hand, instead of a fist."* I bristled, but ignored them, trying to focus on the purpose of the work.

My co-trainer, Dwight Washington, introduced the Cycle of Violence. He spoke of institutional violence and how this tension leads to a reaction of counter violence. The response to reactive violence is often to repress and stifle the expression of tension. This leads back to the original issues of institutional violence, which keeps the cycle going. Dwight then skillfully wove the subject of domestic violence into his presentation as an example, noting the institutional violence of misogyny, sexism, economic disparities, homophobia, anti-Semitism and racism fuel a sense of disempowerment, frustration and anger. This powder keg can lead to reactionary or counter violence, even played out in domestic violence in the home or in relationships with how we talk to one another or treat others. Out of embarrassment or fear, the intense emotions are repressed, allowing the cycle of violence to continue. With his gentle steady introduction to the subject, Dwight essentially shut down the immature behavior of the males who had originally mocked the subject of nonviolence. Without using shame or disparaging remarks toward these young men, Dwight artfully disarmed them while illustrating the nuance of nonviolence. These same young men went on to fully and appropriately participate in the rest of the training.

———

As a trainer for the Meta Peace Team, Dwight notes, *"Responding to violence with violence is like throwing a match into a fire."*[1] With a master's degree in human development and psychology and a Ph.D in natural resources, Dwight focuses his understanding of the human psyche as a county commissioner working for his community. One fall day, we sat at my table and philosophized about the tools of nonviolence, and how *"if the only tool you have is a hammer, then everything looks like a nail."* Dwight expanded on this:

> *If all we have as a country, as a tribe, as a person, is violence, then every time we are afraid or every time there is a disagreement, we use that tool. It is a fight or flight response. It is part of our mammalian brain, but we also have a much larger cerebrum and the ability to choose a different response, to redirect. Meta Peace Team is saying that we don't have to subject ourselves to violence, we don't have to use fire hoses. We can find a different*

*way and change the perspective from fight or flight. These are regular people choosing a different way.* [2]

When rage or anger builds, it is an opportunity to redirect that emotion to more positive and constructive outcomes. Our challenge becomes transforming that intense feeling into a creative power for good. Dwight recalls how he started with Meta Peace Team:

*After getting my master's degree, I started going to various rallies, and it seems MPT was always there. I would watch them from afar. I remember seeing how they interacted with people at the KKK rally in Lansing. The KKK represents such violence, and my life as a black child and now a man had actually been so opposite to them, I wanted to go to the rally to witness. What I saw was people with yellow vests saying 'Peace Team,' interacting and engaging with people, actively listening, placing themselves as a presence in the crowd. I wanted to be part of that.* [3]

Committed to water safety and community development, Dwight was active with many of the MPT trainings held in the Flint area in response to the water crisis when lead in the water poisoned many of the children and their families in the city. It was a service to the community to have the trainings, teaching people the skills of nonviolence, Active Listening, the CLARA method, and Bystander Intervention. The Meta Peace Team was there as Flint residents walked door to door with water bottles and information to organize the community. For Dwight, it was an opportunity to witness the conditions in which the people of Flint were living. There were scattered desolate buildings, burned and abandoned, with random individuals coming into the community to vandalize and take advantage of the victims of the water crisis. Yet, there were many deeply committed people who defended their city, their culture, their children and their health. They held numerous community gatherings with food and festivities to inform the people of the city about their rights, and the process of improving their water supply.

*The people of Flint told us they felt the MPT presence calmed and created security for them going door to door. It was hard to fathom, that myself and a team of senior citizens could be viewed as a security team. But they told us a couple times where they felt our presence made the difference. Mary Ellen Jeffreys and Peter Dougherty are in their 80s, and they get in your face in a nonviolent way. Together, we brought them a sense of security.* [4]

It was Mary Ellen Jeffreys who brought Dwight into MPT, urging his participation and recruiting him for the work of nonviolence, because it is *"the only thing that lasts."* Starting as the custodian for the office where MPT was housed, Mary Ellen has been a consistent behind-the-scenes presence helping MPT exist for the past 25 years. She has organized mailings, helped write fundraising letters, prepared the materials for trainings, and participated in more peace teams than she can name. Of her role, Mary Ellen states, *"I carry the bags."* She "retired" in 2018 at the young age of 84, but remains active on local peace teams. *"It takes all of us to stand up and do something."* [5]

Dwight reminds me of the event in Boston after Charlottesville. Most of the nation was outraged over the images of torches, the injuries and death associated with the Unite the Right rally, when white nationalists marched through the streets of Charlottesville, Virginia, in August 2017. More marches were planned by the so-called Alt-Right groups, including the one in Boston. Forty thousand people were present in a peaceful and steady protest as 100 Alt-Right followers gathered at a gazebo in the park. The peaceful protesters made a statement by standing ceremoniously with their backs to the Alt-Right group. It was a powerful message, and no one was injured. Other rallies planned across the country by the Alt-Right group were canceled because of the counter-protest in Boston. How different would events have been in Charlottesville if thousands of nonviolent activists been there as a peace team? Potentially a peace team presence could have countered the hatred and vitriol percolated by the Alt-Right group in the days leading up to the moment when a neo-Nazi white nationalist drove his car into a group of peaceful protesters and took the life of Heather Heyer.

Dwight notes:

> *A committed band of people can change the world. It would change the world if we could have a Meta Peace Team in every state, go into the schools, businesses, train police forces with the tactics of violence de-escalation and Bystander Intervention. If we had a database with the ability to mobilize our team to be a presence where and when we are needed, it could be a different world.* [6]

As part of Meta Peace Team trainings, there is time set aside for trainers to tell stories of empowerment, with stories of real people doing the work of nonviolence. At a time in our history when ideological divisions are stoked and supported by people in leadership positions, when the economic disparities are growing wider and definitions of "us" and "them" are more entrenched, it is easy to feel powerless and hopeless, as if this vilification is normal. The advent of the twenty-four-hour news cycle and social media add to this powder keg. It seems anger and fear are a daily reaction to the barrage of information coming at us over the airways. But at the heart of who we are as a species is not the competitive violent individual, rather, we are a cooperative species with the capacity for empathy and love. To be human is to be part of a community, we are all part of a family no matter how we define it. In any family, there are challenges and misconduct that can hurt or harm. So too, in the wider family of our state, our nation, and the larger world.

*To be angry at injustice and to fear harm are natural human responses. The point is not whether we have the 'right' to be frightened or outraged but how can we use that fear or outrage to change a situation most effectively.* [7]

———

Every day, people are answering this challenge with their generosity in times of national or international disasters, with wisdom and perspective in times of tragedy, and with nonviolence and civil disobedience in times of injustice. It is imperative to have the successful stories of nonviolence sung from the rooftops, letting us all know the power and possibility of this "third way," beyond violence and beyond passive indifference. This kind of nonviolent change is made by everyday people. Emily Fijol, who was the director of development for the Residential College of Arts and Humanities at Michigan State University before moving on to Ohio State University in October 2019, told me the story of growing up in the sleepy conservative town of Oxford, Ohio, in the 1980s. She recalls that as a child she witnessed the yearly marches of the Ku Klux Klan down Main Street, waving their flags and wearing their hoods. Some townspeople would attend, standing on the side of the street as the marchers passed, chanting slogans and bringing with them an air of dominance, fear, and terror. Each year, it seemed there were fewer and fewer people to watch the parade. Eventually businesses purposely closed on that day, and many townspeople boycotted the area, leaving the KKK alone on their march through town. No one paid any attention to them anymore, so the marches ended around 1986. The nonviolent tactic of boycotting made the difference.

There are stories of everyday people like the nurses who helped a 16-year-old boy from Honduras. He and his father had ridden in the back of a closed truck, smuggled into the country after a dangerous trek through the desert away from the violence and poverty in their homeland. They took a chance and came into the U.S. without permission, choosing to risk dying in the desert rather than dying at the hands of the gangs back home. The temperature in the back of the truck was stifling and many people in their party died of heat exhaustion on the journey. Upon arrival on U.S. soil, the doors of the truck were opened and the carnage was evident. The boy was unconscious and taken to the hospital. His beleaguered father stood at his bedside as nurses worked to gradually bring his body temperature back to normal with cool clothes and hydration. The next day, officers from Immigration and Customs Enforcement arrived to arrest the father and son. The boy's nurse and other nurses on the floor stood linked arm in arm as a barrier between the boy and the ICE officers. Life is life, no matter what country he was from or what he was fleeing. There would be no arrest that day.

Neighborhoods are changed by the actions of everyday people like Laura Ray. She grew up in a neighborhood in Lansing, Michigan, known for its gangs and gang violence. She moved away to go to school, but returned and became a quiet role model; someone who grew up there but "made it." She had gone to college and became a social worker. Laura raised her children in the Baker Street neighborhood, where gunshots were frequently heard, and helicopters sometimes passed overhead scanning backyards with searchlights. The influx of crack changed the dynamics of the gangs, and it has turned "every man for himself." Usually the people of the neighborhood stay to themselves and don't intervene in other people's "business." In 2017, Laura participated in a Meta Peace Team training, and she did not think the strategies would work. With her life experience coming from a place of violence, she was skeptical.

Then one day, she noticed a husband and wife verbally and physically fighting. They were loud and punching and grabbing each other as they made their way down the street. They eventually ended up on Laura's front lawn. Laura went out to interact with the couple, and her husband followed. They pulled the man off his wife and stood between them, speaking in low and firm tones using logic to relate: *"It doesn't have to be like this. The cops are going to come and you could both be in trouble. You can figure out a different way."*

Eventually, the man gave up, and his reasoning returned. Laura recalls feeling surprised with the effectiveness of the intervention she had learned at the MPT training. Her actions gave the fighting couple a chance to make a different choice. When Laura looked up, she saw a handful of teenagers who had been filming the event in the hopes of posting it on Instagram from their phones. She saw a look of disappointment when the interaction was thwarted. Unintentionally, Laura had headed off another problem: the depiction of violence as entertainment on social media. [8] And perhaps she planted a seed of nonviolence in the consciousness of those young people as well.

There are everyday people making a difference within law enforcement. The Crisis Intervention Team is an innovative police-based program for first responders to mental illness and domestic violence crises and 911 calls. Trainees go through an educational and experiential forty-hour training in the skills of violence de-escalation and Active Listening. Once answering a call, the officers are trained to slow down, evaluate, assess, and use their skills to develop rapport. Realizing people with a mental illness are having a medical crisis, often not a criminal crisis, the officers use their skills to avoid using force while reducing the risk of officer injury or incarceration for the offender. Officers feel like they are addressing real issues by putting people in contact with appropriate health services, rather than responding to every call with a ready weapon. Costs to the community are decreased as mental health clients are diverted from the criminal justice system to the care they need, causing a decrease in litigation and jail time. The relationship of the police with their community is improved when violent tragedy is diverted and people are helped.

An incident shared on the NPR program "StoryCorps" [9] illustrates how this approach diffused a potentially lethal situation involving an autistic adult named Walker, who had a serious reaction to his new medication. It caused him to become so agitated and violent that his mother drove him to the hospital. When they arrived at the emergency department, he was thrashing and hitting and eventually bit his mother. Four uniformed officers swarmed around Walker, pinning him to the ground to control him. The mother feared for his life. Suddenly, she heard a steady deep voice approach while calmly saying, *"Walker, put his hands on his head, Walker, put his hands on his hips, Walker, give high-fives to all the guys!"* She looked up at the approaching man, who was Officer Keith. She saw a smile spread across Walker's face as he followed the instructions. Officer Keith then started singing "Mr. Rogers Neighborhood" and the mother watched as her son relaxed with the instructions from Officer Keith, singing along with him. Having an autistic son himself, Officer Keith knew how to handle this situation without violence. Using more tools than their weapons can rapidly change the dynamic of a situation, in many cases for the better.

The owner of Schertzing Communications, Nancy Schertzing, is an everyday person who has embraced an alternative to punishment, which often perpetuates the cycle of violence. She teaches Restorative Justice in educational settings and leads interventions across the state of Michigan. Nancy tells the story of two friends who lived next door to each other. Lisa was in sixth grade and Sami was in eighth grade. Their younger siblings were best friends and their mothers often got together socially. One day while walking home from school, Lisa walked up to Sami and hit her, threw her to the ground and started beating her. The moms were outraged, forbidding their children to interact with each other again, as the altercation essentially destroyed their relationship. The two girls and their moms were invited to participate in Restorative Justice. Each participant was allowed to speak uninterrupted, to tell their side of what happened and how they had been affected by the event. Then each participant was asked to define how the harm could be healed and the role each would play in the healing. When asked what happened, Lisa noted the vitriolic cyber bullying from Sami, and one day she just couldn't take it anymore and unfortunately reacted with violence toward her neighbor. Suddenly, the offender was the victim, and the victim was the offender. The participants in the circle bravely brainstormed on the actions that needed to be taken to heal this harm. Finally, Lisa looked at her mom and said, "I think you moms need to apologize to each other, too." There was silence, then there was nervous laughter, then there was sincere apology. It was a powerful interaction. Nancy summarizes the work of Restorative Justice:

> *These skills, this philosophy, this paradigm can be used in any situation, any relationship. When you cause harm, you can heal it. Rather than vilifying, accusing, demanding, demonizing, or expecting someone else to fix it, we can use Restorative Justice techniques. So much of crime and punishment is based on fear. In looking for ways to heal even horrific crimes, there is a humane way much more productive than punishment, which is further harming. If we're looking to heal, there is nothing to be afraid of. It is so freeing.* [10]

There are voices of everyday people like Barbara Harvey and members of the Jewish Voice for Peace, who are trying to help Americans understand the need for better relations between Israelis and Palestinians. Their mission statement notes:

> *Jewish Voice for Peace opposes anti-Jewish, anti-Muslim, and*

*anti-Arab bigotry and oppression. JVP seeks an end to the Israeli occupation of the West Bank, Gaza Strip, and East Jerusalem; security and self-determination for Israelis and Palestinians; a just solution for Palestinian refugees based on principles established in international law; an end to violence against civilians; and peace and justice for all peoples of the Middle East. (Adopted in 2009)* [11]

It is a grassroots activist movement empowering people to action.

*We seek to be accountable to those directly affected by Israel's discriminatory and violent policies and practices, while working to effectively build and accountably deploy our power as American Jews.* [12]

Their actions include the dissemination of information, and stories of the treatment of Palestinians in the Israeli occupied territories. Inspired by Mahatma Gandhi, Martin Luther King Jr., and the U.S. civil rights movement, the people of Jewish Voice for Peace support the nonviolent path to justice through the Palestinian BDS movement, which includes Boycott, Divestment, and Sanctions. They focus on the problem, not the people. While not opposing Jewish people, BDS opposes the Israeli state policies and practices that maintain widespread discrimination against the Palestinian people, affecting all the people of the region. Addressing various businesses whose products or investments support the occupation, the use of BDS actions have been working to make change. BDS investment groups are asking computer giants, for instance, to stop development of biometric identification devices and invisible fences because it helps maintain the police state in Palestine. Construction moguls are boycotted for supplying bulldozers that are used to tear down Palestinian homes. When products are boycotted, when divestment is demanded and sanctions are upheld, pressure is applied and often gets results in a nonviolent way. Unfortunately, supporters of BDS are labeled anti-Semitic, when in fact they are working for justice, equality and dignity for all people. In her speech at the Women's March in Detroit in 2019, Barbara said:

> *Tyranny is a path that leads to the edge of the cliff. The position of Jewish Voice for Peace springs from love for brethren in Israel who have lost their way and for the Palestinian community we have come to know, admire, and respect. Israel asserts a status as 'the Jewish state' to argue that criticism of Israel is anti-Semitic. This is ridiculous. No country is entitled to a free ride to injustice and tyranny.* [13]

Barbara Harvey recalls her trip to the Gaza Strip in 1986. As a Jewish American, she wanted to see first-hand the effects of the Israeli-Palestinian conflict. It was a ten-day trip during which she saw the resilience and the generosity of the Palestinian people. She saw the deterioration of the Palestinian society which prior to the occupation was known as one of the most literate societies in the world. Now, just getting through high school is a nonviolent resistance to the occupation. One of the last days of the trip, Barbara and her group went to Jabalia refugee camp. At the time it was a spacious place but has since been reduced to rubble with the multiple bombings. Their group visited an embroidery room, where many teens were learning the old-style art of needlepoint.

> *I hadn't told anyone I was Jewish on the trip; I was dealing with too much so I had not disclosed this to anyone. But on this last day, I thought I would try it. I was talking through an interpreter with one of the young women, and I told her, 'I am an American Jew.' As the interpretation sank in, I never anticipated what happened. This poor young woman, once she understood what I had said, she looked at me with terror in her eyes. She was trembling with fear. No one had ever responded to me like that in my life. Once I collected myself, I told the interpreter, 'please tell her that*

*I am not here as her enemy, I am here as her friend and I am here to help.' When the translator finished, this terrified young girl who had every right to respond with hatred, she started to cry and then she embraced me. I was so moved that she could respond with such love to a member of the oppressor group. I knew, as I had seen through the entire trip, that these are not animals, these are not terrorists. These are wonderful people who are being stomped on.* (14)

We are all everyday people. We are all capable of making the choice for nonviolence. We can start with how we talk to each other. In his seminal book, *Nonviolent Communication*, the late Marshall B. Rosenberg lays out the four components of Nonviolent Communication: observation, feelings, needs, and requests. In a back-and-forth flow of communication, we can name the concrete actions we OBSERVE that affect our well-being, then tell how we FEEL in relation to what we observe. Follow this with the NEEDS, values, desires, etc. that create our feelings, and give concrete actions we REQUEST in order to enrich our lives. (15) I remember at my first MPT training, trainer Katie Ames was demonstrating the use of personal power messages, known as I-statements. She told about an intervention she recalled with a couple of neighborhood boys who were throwing trash down the sewer grate on her street. There is symmetry in the "recipe" for this nonviolent communication and personal power messages using I-statements, what I like to call I-own-it statements.

For instance:

*I see you throwing garbage down the sewer (OBSERVE), and I feel worried this could plug up the drain and cause a backflow of rainwater (FEEL). I value the environment and a clean street (NEED), so I'd like you to throw the garbage in the garbage can instead of the sewer (REQUEST).*

We brainstormed with other scenarios where this style of communication could be more effective than our usual finger-pointing — or You-statements. For instance, upon arrival at a friend's house you see the kitchen in disarray, knowing there has been some stressful times in the past few months. How can we voice our concern without being judgmental?

*I see the pile of dishes and the numerous empty wine bottles on your counter (OBSERVE), and I feel concerned the drinking may be used to deal with some of the stress (FEEL). I want you to be content and healthy (NEED), so I wonder if you'd tell me how you're feeling. What's going on for you? (REQUEST)*

In the lunchroom at work, there are some workmates who are using disparaging language about gays and lesbians. What can we say that communicates our discomfort?

*I hear the derogatory language toward gays and lesbians (OBSERVE), and I feel hurt because I have relatives and friends who are gay (FEEL). I would like to be in a friendship with you (NEED), so please don't refer to my family and friends with such a negative tone (REQUEST).*

An elderly relative makes a comment that she is running out of her medication but because of the weather, she cannot get to the pharmacy. "Oh well, I guess I will just go without it." It is her usual way of asking for help.

*I hear an indirect request from you (OBSERVE), and I feel a sense of guilt which makes me feel uncomfortable (FEEL). I need to feel better about my interactions with you (NEED), so I would like to be directly asked for help when you need it (REQUEST).*

Upon arriving at work, the medical assistant notices a mess at her desk, which she had left orderly the day before. The physician with whom she works had used her desk area and left it in disarray. Rather than stuffing the anger she feels inside, she can own her feelings and set some boundaries.

> *When I arrived this morning, my desk was a mess and my things were not in order (OBSERVE). I feel disorganized and this makes it harder for me to do my job (FEEL). I need an orderly work environment so I can be efficient (NEED), so if you use my desk area, please leave it as neat as you found it (REQUEST).*

Anytime we need to have potentially difficult conversations, using I-own-it statements allows a positive environment without creating an adversarial interaction where self-defense is often the reaction.

> *I have been completing my work as well as the work of people not replaced in the office (OBSERVE). I feel proud of the value I add to the office and the product we produce (FEEL). I need to be recognized for this value, and in our line of work this recognition is shown with financial remuneration (NEED), so I am asking for the following increase in my salary..... (REQUEST)*

We can focus our communication with one another in a nonviolent way, using these I-own-it statements. We own what we Observe and what we Feel, and by verbalizing our Needs, we naturally make a reasonable Request. This type of communication is less likely to create a response of defensiveness, embarrassment or shame, which in some circumstances escalates to violence. This strategy can start a dialogue while creating a safe space for the other party who can then share their observations, feelings, needs, and requests as well. It is a skill that can be learned and practiced. How different the world could be if we started with nonviolent communications with each other.

Realistically, we can follow these suggestions being conscious of using I-statements, personal power messages, and actively listening, but still be met with hard-headed, guilt-ridden or violent responses. Just because we speak our truth doesn't mean anyone will listen. We can hope people do the right thing, but sometimes they don't. We can have the general expectation that people will do good, and it is painful when they choose otherwise. Katie Ames shares the story of growing up in a violently abusive home. She recalls being 10 years old and understanding that people who grow up in abuse are likely to repeat it. The oppressed often become the oppressor. She had a conversation with herself:

> *Katie, you have a choice. You can go with the flow and turn out the same way or you can find another way. I could see how I was physically and emotionally reacting to the violence in my home and I didn't want this for my life. I knew I didn't have any control over the situation, but I had control over my reactions to it.* [16]

She set out to do what she could to deal with the dysfunctions in her home. When she felt the rage inside her, she would focus on doing something physical. She figured out how to redirect the power of the anger inside her by doing chores. No parent ever suspected this was a coping strategy, but it worked as an outlet for the tumult inside her. She also looked for positive role models by reading Ann Landers, talking with teachers or the mothers of her friends. She knew she needed to connect with other adults in a positive way.

> *I was so determined. I wanted something different and I knew I wasn't going to get it from my family, so I asked myself, 'What am I going to do?' I had to make it happen. I am still making it happen. Anyone who grows up in abuse knows it affects everything. We can choose to hurt or heal, to harm or help. We have the power for each, whether we choose it or not. I often tell people, 'You can make a different choice.'* [17]

Hearing stories from her dad of comradery with his platoon in Vietnam, Katie joined the Army as a way to serve her country and to honor the men who didn't come home. She served in the Army for nine years, with four of those years on active duty in Germany and at Fort Benning. She recalls struggling with the reality of her decision to join the Army when a rifle was first placed in her hands. Even now that she has been out of service for almost twenty years, she admits she has an "existential angst" when she realizes that she has the skills and knowledge to kill somebody, and to do it without thinking.

> *I am not afraid of dying, but I am afraid of killing. I am afraid of doing harm. I know what it feels like to get to that edge and have to make a split-second decision which could change things forever. I have spent a lifetime trying to find peaceful ways, but from my background with abuse I know how you can get to that rage and go over the edge to the wrong side. I am diligently and constantly working on peaceful ways because I want that to be my automatic response.* [18]

Individuals are changed by the choices they make. Katie's life was changed when she made the choice to do it differently than what she had been shown. As an adult, she has made the choice to focus on the healing rather than the harming, on the helping rather than the hurting. Skills taught by the Meta Peace Team can support the decision to be nonviolent with words and actions. It can be a romantic and grandiose idea to go out into the world and make a big difference as a "peacemaker," but the work is really a quiet daily decision within each one of us. Who do we want to be?

Katie reflects on her life:

> *If I am struggling with someone, or I get mad or pissed off and want to strike out, I pause and look in the mirror and ask myself, 'Who do you want to be?' It stops me in my tracks. I need to*

*decide how to maintain the person I want to be. I always have a choice. Sometimes there is time to think about it and sometimes we have to make a quick decision, but we always have a choice. We may be in a physical situation we can't change but we can change how we react to it."* (19)

Whether it is at school, at work, at the Thanksgiving dinner table, or any time we are presented with people who look different than we do, believe different than we do, vote different than we do — or quite frankly piss us off in any way — we have a choice. We can respond with the same harmful words and deeds that feed the otherization in our world, or we can learn and practice the abundant tools in the nonviolent toolbox, realizing it holds much more than a hammer. It holds Active Listening, I-own-it state-ments, Nonviolent Communication strategies, Restorative Justice, Bystander Intervention tactics, and the CLARA method. These skills are tools that strengthen individuals, families, communities, and our wider society. We just have to use them.

*Children making the peace sign*

CONCLUSION

# SHINE THE LIGHT

*The world is before you*
*and you need not take it or leave it*
*as it was when you came in.*
*—James Baldwin*

It seems there is an archetypal struggle between "us" and "them," between "kin" and "other." The examples of these struggles are numerous throughout time, and in just focusing on the short history of America we find plenty. The English settlers colonizing the New World, demonizing the Native Americans whose land they took. The Colonists and the Loyalists in the Revolutionary War with the tarring and feathering of enemies. The battle between the competing interests of the North and the South during the Civil War. The reactionary Jim Crow laws, which forbade interracial marrying, restricted voting rights, and allowed the continuation of the abuse of black bodies with lynching and rape. The tide of immigrants flooding into America in pursuit of a dream, but still the fighting between Catholics and Protestants, Poles and Germans, Italians and Russians. The push and pull between unions and corporate bosses for fair wages, fair hours, fair labor laws. The consistent struggle for women's rights: to vote, to determine the boundaries of their own bodies, to receive an equal wage for equal work. Placing lives on the line for civil rights as people ask to be valued for the content of their character rather than the color of their skin. Evolving to an understanding that love is love, no matter what the gender or sexual identity. And the demonization continues as refugees from poverty and war-torn countries seek asylum at our borders to this day. We are always trying to find a balance between progressing to a new understanding and conserving the known ways. We do not live in a vacuum, what affects one directly, affects all indirectly.

Perhaps it is part of our mammalian brain that we separate ourselves into tribes and sometimes fight to the death. But an opposable thumb is not the only thing that separates us from our mammal friends; we have a cerebral cortex and the ability to think abstractly, to learn new concepts and to make choices. For instance, we happen to be surrounded by sugar and processed foods and need to make a daily decision on what we feed our physical body in order for it to operate and feel its best. We also happen to be surrounded by messages of fear and hate. But there are many examples of love, kindness, generosity, and aid. Again, we need to make a daily choice of what to feed our mind and our soul, to operate and be our best. Our choices are important when answering the question, "Who do I want to be?"

One of my favorite storytellers is Rachel Naomi Remen MD. She was diagnosed with Crohn's disease at the age of 15, and her experiences with that disease have shaped her identity and strengthened her ability to help others. She tells the story her beloved orthodox rabbi grandfather told her. It is called The Birthday of the World.

*In the beginning, there was only the holy darkness, known as Ein Sof, the 'source of life.' Then in the course of history, at a moment in time this world emerged from the heart of the holy darkness as a great ray of light. And then, there was an accident. And the vessels containing the light of the world, the wholeness of the world, broke. And the wholeness of the world, the light of the world, was scattered into a thousand-thousand fragments of light. And they fell into all events and all people, where they remain deeply hidden until this very day.*

*Now, according to my grandfather, the whole human race is a response to this accident. We are here because we are born with the capacity to find the hidden light in all events and all people; to lift it up and make it visible once again and, thereby, to restore the innate wholeness of the world. This task is called 'tikkun olam' in Hebrew, 'restoring the world.' We heal the world one heart at a time. It involves all people who have ever been born, all people presently alive, and all people yet to be born. We are all healers of the world.*

*It is a very old story. It's a different way of looking at our power. We could feel that we're not enough to make a difference; that we need to be more, somehow, either wealthier or more educated or, somehow or other different than the people we are. We ask ourselves, 'How can I make a difference when I am so wounded?' But according to this story, we are exactly what's needed. It's our very wounds that enable us to make a difference. We are the right people, just as we are.* [1]

In her book, *Kitchen Table Wisdom*, Remen tells another story that has become my guiding light, and I use it often when I teach. It is a story of a young man who loses his leg to osteogenic sarcoma bone cancer, saving his life yet ending it as he knew it. Having once been an athlete, he is despondent and now feels himself worthless. During a counseling session, he draws himself as a beautiful vase with a huge crack down the middle, angrily drawing over and over the crack with the crayon clenched in his hand. He describes himself as the vase, once able to hold colorful flowers but now broken and unable to do what it was meant to do. As he struggles to find meaning and purpose in his life, he eventually volunteers at the hospital to help others. There, he meets a young woman who has just had a mastectomy. Finding her depressed and unmoved by his attempts to get her to smile, he finally removes his artificial leg and starts dancing on one leg. The woman finally laughs, and says, *"Fella, if you can dance, then maybe I can sing."*

Back in counseling the young man asks for his drawing of the vase. He takes a yellow crayon from the box and draws streams of light radiating from the crack to the edges of the paper. Pointing to the crack, he quietly said, *"this is where the light comes through."* [2]

We all have cracks in our vase from which our light can shine and connect to others. When we tell our stories, we understand we are not alone and our lights can start that connection. It is in the telling of stories that we see ourselves and can start to see others as kin. Stories tell us who we are, what is possible for us, and what we can call upon in our challenges. Stories remind us we are connected to each other and to resources within ourselves and the larger world that may be supporting us in our struggles. In the telling of stories, we are given the gift of possibility; the ability to see what is possible, both positively and negatively. Then it is up to us to choose which wolf to feed.

The stories in this book have been an effort at *tikkun olam*. It is an effort to "restore the world" by telling stories of people who are using their light to connect to each other and make a difference in the world. Having come from an alcoholic home, Reverend Peter Dougherty chose to learn the skills of nonviolence and has dedicated his life's work to teaching, preaching and walking this talk. Jasiu Milanowski used his *Satyagraha*, or truth-force, in his civil disobedience actions for nuclear disarmament. The work of the Meta Peace Team they founded is an inoculation against violence, and people like Mary Hanna show up every day to make this happen. The light of Kim Redigan is evident as she takes students into a place of seeing, knowing, and understanding the injustices of our world, and how they can make it just. Marginalized populations are given a voice and sometimes a home with the actions of

Sheri Wander, as she works to dismantle the Cage of Oppression. It is a perennial goal to loosen the chains of apartheid in the Israeli/Palestinian conflict, with the eventual goal of removing the chains altogether by the work of Elliott Adams, Linda Sartor, Barbara Harvey and so many others. It is evident in the hundreds of volunteers who show up every day at the U.S./Mexico border, attempting to "love thy neighbor." It is also the thousands of everyday people who choose not to be complicit, by utilizing skills of Bystander Intervention when they see or hear harm happening.

It is the "thousand points of light" so aptly phrased by President George H.W. Bush when he spoke of America. [3] We can extend this to the world and speak of millions of points of light, knowing that we all have the capacity to find the hidden light in all people and all events. It takes great courage and a willingness to sit with our vulnerability when we reach out to connect with others, especially those we have traditionally viewed as "other." And it takes patience and practice to choose a response other than violence when we feel afraid or threatened. We can transform our animalistic modus operandi into something stronger and more lasting. *"Nonviolence is not really the recourse of the weak, but actually calls upon the uncommon kind of strength; it is not a refraining from something, but the engaging of a positive force."* [4] It is choosing not to fight, not to flee, but to stand as a force of nonviolence to change the situation.

Where do we go from here? Often when actions for change are listed in books, lectures, or seminars, "self-care" is usually saved for last and given a tacit mention at best. But self-care is a place to start in the work of nonviolence. It is vital to become grounded in our own personal and spiritual self-care, which is essential when doing any nonviolent work. It can maintain us while we utilize these skills in challenging situations. Everyone defines self-care for themselves, thus the term "self" care. For some this includes exercise, yoga, prayer, or meditation. For others, self-care includes expression through art, music, dance, gardening, singing, etc. We are more grounded when we allow joy and playfulness, seek opportunities for laughter and welcome levity to balance the heaviness of life.

Then, it seems we need to start seeing each other as human, rather than demonizing and denying the humanity of others. The Native American people were labeled "savages" and often depicted as such in movies and literature. Tragically, their demonization more easily allowed the usurpation of their land and tribal traditions. Slaves were listed as three-fifths a human, shackled like cattle, and sold to the highest bidder. Defining slaves as property allowed the dehumanizing economic argument to win the day. Upon reflection of the concentration camps and the treatment of Jews in the Holocaust, Nazi soldiers often admitted they did not see the Jews as human, rather as animals. No doubt, by denying their humanity, it was easier to deny their right to exist. Now, our leaders call immigrants and those seeking asylum from troubled homelands "aliens," as if from another planet and undeserving of basic human rights and needs such as shelter, food, education and medical care. Words and labels have power and create energy that ripples outward like water after a pebble is thrown. Each of us has a choice in the words we speak, and the voice we use in response to dehumanizing language. Using the skills of Bystander Intervention, we can intervene to change the demonizing tone when we hear it.

We could all benefit from a healthier diet, especially the diet of information we take in every day. "The News" used to be Walter Cronkite at six o'clock every night telling us "and that's the way it is." There were three major networks and all had local, state, and federal news in a sixty-minute time slot. People tuned in, got their daily dose, then went on with their daily living. Now, there are too many news stations to count, delivering the same recycled commentary over and over to fill a twenty-four-hour cycle, hyping even the most mundane of snow falls into a blizzard. The vitriolic language and demonization of people from a different ideological slant is commonplace and has fed the culture of contempt in which we now find ourselves, further polarizing us from each other. It is a psychological warfare tactic used to manipulate masses of people, and it works. Each of us has a choice in how we use media, how varied are our sources for information, how often we check our phones, how often we turn off the TV or the computer, and how we check for validity in a story.

As consumers, we have power in what we consume both informationally and nutritionally, and change happens when we change. At the risk of sounding naïve, I believe if we heard more stories of the goodness in humanity, we would race to the top to be part of it. Instead, it seems there is a resurgence of individualistic supremacy rather than seeing all our boats tied to each other. If the only thing we hear all day are stories of man's inhumanity to man, it is easy to feel emotions of fear, sadness, hopelessness and grief. If we hear stories of people's generosity and service to each other, it is easier to feel hope, joy, and potential. We have always taught our children, "you get what you give." So, be kind and you will usually get kindness in return. The other is also true; we give what we get when it comes to the barrage of negative information in our diet. It creates an anxious, irritable response in our gut and we react in our life accordingly. We can make a different choice.

I remember in history class being instructed with the phrase, "those who don't learn history are doomed to repeat it." But it seems that's all we do — repeat history with wars and fighting and hurting time and time again. Our nation's capital has many beautiful monuments and statues, but there is only one monument which honors peace: the Martin Luther King Jr. monument. The honoring of those fallen in war is important, but focusing only on the tool of violence does a disservice to the men and women who helped make great change in America through civil disobedience and Active Nonviolence. There is great skill, great courage, and great effort needed in the work of nonviolence, and the stories of this work and its successes need to be told, learned, and honored. Instead, we use the same tools and strategies of war and violence despite research noting the more lasting effects of nonviolent campaigns. Albert Einstein is credited with exclaiming, *"the definition of insanity is doing the same thing over and over again, and expecting different results."* We won't solve our problems with the same mindset that created them. The skills of Active Nonviolence can be more routinely taught, and the tools in our tool belt can be varied.

Curriculums at all educational levels could include lessons for Active Listening, Nonviolent Communication, Bystander Intervention, and emotional intelligence development. From grade school, to middle school, to high school and beyond, including these lessons as a regular part of our education can improve classroom cultures, increase student performance, decrease challenging behavior such as bullying, and support a healthier citizenry. Using creativity and innovative ideas enables this to become a regular part of every school day.

Thinking of grade school aged children, I remember my own kids growing up. As parents, we teach our children the definitions of words and their applications. We define the world for them. This is a tree, this is a chair, this is a spoon, and this is what we do with a spoon, etc. It is also important that we define emotion, demonstrating and role modeling how it is expressed, how it affects us and those around us. This is happy, this is sad, this is grief, this is anger, and this is how we express it, etc. In my experience, we consciously define words, but we unconsciously define emotions and how we use them. If we more consciously teach our children the words and expression of emotion, we could all develop more healthy and appropriate ways to express ourselves.

When my son was 4 years old, we often went to the school playground in our neighborhood. He was swinging and watching as other families came out to relish one of the first warm days of spring. He ran off to play on the slide, and when he came back to the swing, someone else was using it. He stopped in his tracks and stared at the boy. I stood watching him, seeing the inner conflict brewing inside him. We had been conscious of teaching him how to handle anger by stomping his feet, rather than the usual temper tantrum of the age. My son paused, looked at me, then looked back at the boy on the swing, and stomped his foot. I yelped, *"That's it! That's what you do when you're angry!"* Feeling satisfied, he grinned and ran off to play on something else at the playground. It felt like a lesson for a lifetime clicked in those few seconds.

Education starts at home, but is supplemented, supported and expanded with school curriculums. As children progress through elementary school armed with the language of emotion and potentially schooled in the skills of Active Listening, they enter the tumultuous middle school years. Their bodies are growing and changing but their minds are also expanding to understand themselves, others and their place in the world. This time of rapid growth needs edges and support to guide young people to their best selves. Like cells that grow rapidly, without the checks and balances of the immune system those cells can become cancerous. Parents, teachers and mentors are the checks and balances for the adolescent and their rapid growth physically, emotionally, mentally, and spiritually. Investing in social-emotional learning programs is an inoculation against self-harm, acting out, bullying and other forms of violence as students develop tools for coping with the challenges in their lives.

Moving through high school and beyond, the challenges start to include career goals, further education, developing sexuality and identity; all while balancing family, friends, social media, and the potential for various substances that can place a road block on their path of becoming. This is a time of great potential for incorporating the use of personal power messages/I-statements and

Active Listening as tools for interactions with peers, educators, parents and the greater society. Beyond the reading, writing, and arithmetic, student development is enriched by programs which guide their understanding of themselves; the role of privilege, the effects of systemic violence in the form of racism, sexism, ableism, classism, etc. Programs like Intergroup Dialogues are invited into classrooms to give students the opportunity to understand the unconscious use of labels and the language of "otherism," which often creates the coals of anger which smolder, setting the stage and fueling the cycle of violence. Role plays are utilized to practice the skills of developing a new way to interact and speak, so we can be heard without harming. My daughter was part of this educational program at Michigan State University and her learning has rippled into our family, enhancing our understanding of bias and its effects on the cycle of violence. According to Donna Kaplowitz, Ph.D, a leading educator in the Intergroup Dialogues, *"The impact of participating gives students the skills needed to interrupt bias and become leaders in school and in their lives as they become better communicators."* [5] Teaching the skills of Effective Communication throughout the entire educational experience is an important and vital choice we, as a society, need to support if we are to chip away at the systemic violence in our culture.

The Meta Peace Team is just one of many groups that are building new tools of communication and teaching the strategies of nonviolence. Schools are coloring outside the lines, creatively trying new ways to connect with students and the lives they bring to the classroom, in order to optimize their learning. Community service activists have always been and continue to be called upon to provide for the least among us. Many religious groups respond to the prayer of St. Francis of Assisi who asked to *"make me a channel of your peace,"* and actively address the human conditions of hunger, injury, despair, and hatred. Visionary business leaders are stepping forward with innovative cooperative models, empowering many with the potential of greater success for all. Law enforcement is realizing the need to foster community relationships built on trust and respect for the safety of all involved. Citizens are waking up to the role they need to play in a government that is of, by, and for the people. The tool box is getting bigger, and we all have a role to play in using new tools effectively. As penned by Ralph Waldo Emerson, *"The mind, once stretched by a new idea, never returns to its original dimensions."*

We can move beyond the brokenness, beyond the hedonistic, militaristic, authoritarian approach, which has persistently provided the fuel for oppression, anger and reactive violence. We can move beyond the same answers to the same questions, expecting a different outcome but getting what we have always gotten in the cycle of violence. We can listen. We can reflect what we hear to make sure we got it right, and work until we do. We can own our observations, our feelings, our needs and make reasonable requests with the consciousness of nonviolent communication. We can speak up if we hear or see something as a bystander, letting our fellow citizens know they are not alone and we are no longer complicit in their abuse. We can learn more about the skills of Third Party Nonviolent Intervention, or Unarmed Civilian Protection and participate on peace teams domestically and in areas of conflict throughout the world. We can focus on our circle of influence and do all we can, with what we have, in the place we are, with the time we have.

What if …. every class curriculum included developmentally appropriate communications skills in Active Listening, Nonviolent Communication, and Bystander Intervention strategies.

What if …. alongside the disciplinary office in every school there was an office for Restorative Justice, guiding students to a resolution that is fair and just, rather than strictly punitive.

What if …. basic requirements for every college degree included a class in Intercultural Dialogues, not only in the humanities but in business, medicine, engineering, and political science.

What if …. every police department included a Crisis Intervention Team with resources and support for mental health issues and addiction rehabilitation, thereby answering every call with a bigger tool belt holding more tools than a weapon.

What if …. there was an organized Peace Force with hubs in every state, fashioned like the National Guard in that it could be called upon as needed to be a presence in places of potential conflict and violence.

What if …. the U.S. foreign policy supported the people of Israel but rejected the apartheid treatment of the Palestinian people by the Israeli military and the reactionary violent response from Hamas.

What if …. we exported and supported trainings in the skills of Active Nonviolence in countries like El Salvador, Honduras, Venezuela, Cameroon, etc, so their people could rise up and create change in a nonviolent way rather than continue to face the need to escape violence and seek asylum elsewhere.

What if …. the light inside each of us starts to connect one to the other, and we see each other more as kin.

If we arm our children with these skills, we help support tomorrow's citizens as they enter roles of responsibility and leadership. In teaching these skills, we ourselves learn their power, their energy, their effect in our own lives and the lives around us. I believe there would be less gun violence, as there would be other tools to process the deep emotions and vulnerabilities that lead to the use of a gun. I believe there would be less sexual violence, as the use of personal power messages and listening would foster a relationship of respect rather than domination and control. I believe there would be less vitriolic language used to disparage our neighbors, as we see others as humans with similar wounds, similar hopes, and a similar desire to be heard. I believe there would be less self-harm, as we start to see the part we play in *tikkun olam,* our role in restoring the world with our own unique and valuable light. We all have the capacity to see the light in every event and in every person, and we all have the ability to let our light shine through the cracks. In listening to each other's stories, we connect our lights. Though many, we are one. It does not negate the individual, rather, it enhances the power and brilliance of each person. It is not an oversight that at the founding of the United States of America, the national motto was chosen: *E pluribus unum.* To restore the world, *out of many, one.*

We are still called to the challenge of *E pluribus unum.* As one human family, we are not called to sameness but rather to honor our differences and learn to listen to each other and feel heard in our trials and in our triumphs. We are called to dismantle the oppressive labels and empower people to be their best selves. We are called to recognize the cycle of violence and interrupt it with the actions of many as a nonviolent, bold, creative force. We are called to a sense of kinship with each other, which leads to the realization of "justice for all." Then, and only then, it seems, is peace really possible.

In the iconic lyrics written by Dino Valenti and made famous by The Youngbloods:

> *Love is but a song we sing*
> *Fear's the way we die ...*
> *You hold the key to love and fear*
> *All in your trembling hand*
> *Just one key unlocks them both*
> *It's there at your command."* [6]

To unlock love, the key is nonviolence.

*At a Meta Peace Team training, participants witness a role play to learn the skills of Active Non-violence.*

*Peter Dougherty and the peace team at the Republican National Convention in Minneapolis, MN 2008.*

# TRAINING

*...violence is an ugly thing and in the calmer moments
I racked my brains for other ways to get what I wanted.
Better a brain than a fist. A brain can hold anything,
from giant things like distant stars and planets, to tiny
things we can't see, like germs ... A brain can hold a whole
universe, a fist just holds what little it can grab. Or hits
what it can't. — C.A. Fletcher*

I participated in the Meta Peace Team training in March 2017, which was led by Reverend Peter Dougherty, along with Dwight Washington and Katie Ames as co-trainers. There were about twenty of us, mostly from the Lansing and Flint areas of Michigan, and we sat in a circle of chairs. After getting to know each other, we were acquainted with the goals of the day: 1) to understand the power of nonviolence, 2) to learn more about the role of peace teams domestically and internationally, 3) to practice the skills of nonviolence with each other.

Our first lesson included the "Continuum of Violence." On one side of the room was a sign printed "Nonviolent" and on the other side of the room was a sign printed "Violent." The trainers each read a statement, and we had to position ourselves along the continuum where we felt the statement reflected our view of the action as violent or nonviolent. The first statement was:

*Demonstrators smash the windows of a police car after police have been physically abusive to nonviolent protesters.*

Slowly, people started to position themselves along the continuum. We then explained why we stood where we stood. Those who felt it was violent noted the destruction of property, and even though the police were abusive to nonviolent protesters, two wrongs don't make a right. Some people stood close to the middle, feeling the challenge of those abused despite their nonviolent approach and striking out because of it. There weren't any people on the Nonviolent end of the continuum.

The second action statement was:

*Spray painting 'This insults women!' on a sexist billboard.*

Again people started moving, this time toward the Nonviolent end of the continuum. Some stayed on the Violent end, again citing destruction of property, but those on the Nonviolent end of the continuum thought the spray painting was a nonviolent response to the violence of sexism and misrepresentation of women. As people spoke, some adjusted their position to reflect their change of view. Other action statements were:

*A local company present in the community for the past forty years, lays off 300 employees to move the jobs to Mexico.*

*A lumber company clear cuts the trees on the side of a mountain, visible to the roads and city below.*

*Sharing information on Facebook, and the comments are inflammatory and vitriolic name-calling, from both sides of the issue.*

*Animal testing for the manufacturing of makeup. What if it was animal testing used to make medication? What if that medication is used to treat the illness or disease of a loved one in your family?*

Each time, people took positions along the continuum, and each time the comments created movement. The discussion included the discomfort of dealing with degrees of violence, who started the violence, and what recourse people have in the face of violence. Is violence only physical, or is it economic, emotional, mental? Is violence only against a live person, or is it against the environment, a company, a potential? Is it violence when it comes from a faceless person on social media? Is violent action sanctioned when that action goes against something destructive in and of itself? For instance, would it be wrong to take a sledge hammer to dismantle the gas chambers of concentration camps, or nuclear missiles? Each is destruction of property, but where does "violent" end and "nonviolent" begin? Is it ever black and white, or was this an exercise in grayness? We returned to our seats thinking this was murkier than we had expected.

We spent the rest of the morning reviewing communication skills, starting with Active Listening. This type of listening isn't antagonistic, autobiographical or resolution oriented, but rather involves empathy toward another person. It is a method of enhancing interactions. Active Listening is designed to establish and maintain communication of emotions between individuals in a non-judgmental accepting way, without trying to solve the problem, or alter behavior. This skill allows each individual the right to his or her own problems and feelings, and the right to discover his or her own solutions. And although this sounds so lovely and possible, it is all too easy to fall into the argument, or the fix-it mode, or the telling of one's own experience rather than truly listening to another.

For instance, imagine running into a friend at a social function.

People are milling around chatting and eating hors d'oeuvres. You share a story with your friend about a challenging co-worker who is often on her cell phone and isn't pulling her weight in the office. Different types of listening can occur, leading to different types of responses:

*Well, everyone has cell phones, it's just the way it is, so get used to it.*

*Hey, I have someone at my office who does that too! We had to start leaving our phones in a basket at the door and pick them up at the end of our shift, it got so bad.*

*Why don't you just confront them and tell them how much it bothers you, and maybe they'll stop. If not, I'd tell the boss.*

With each example — antagonistic, autobiographical, and resolution oriented — there isn't much listening going on, and it's probably safe to say you don't feel heard. Often this leads to silence and the end of the conversation. There is no connection.

Active Listening is empathic listening and uses body language to signify we are paying attention, focused on the other person. We try to hear the emotion behind what they are saying and then put it into our own words to reflect back to the person what we heard. We aren't trying to fix the problem or sympathize with them by jumping into their problem to wallow with them. Rather, we are interpreting their words, their body language, and putting it into our own words to let them know we heard them. An Active Listener could respond to the case above by asking more questions to clarify the issue, then potentially saying,

*It sounds like you're pretty frustrated. I know you love your work, but it probably adds more to your already full load. How are you handling that?*

196

If someone said this to you, there could then be a clarification of how you feel if it isn't frustrated, and there is an opportunity to expand on what is going on in your life. There is a connection occurring, an interchange of story and emotion and response. It is the beginning of real communication, rather than an end in itself. It is the type of listening where one feels heard. Active Listening is a skill, one that can be learned, and needs to be practiced time and again. It is "conscious" listening, conscious of the other person and what they are saying or trying to say.

Another effective communication tool is referred to as "I-statements" or "Personal Power Messages." Unlike You-statements, an I-statement takes responsibility and ownership for what is said. You-statements can be thought of as pointing a finger at someone, whereas I-statements put a hand over the heart and own the statement or the emotion. I like to think of these as "I-own-it" messages, for I own my perceptions, my feelings, my needs, which I then use to make a request which naturally comes from these. For instance:

I feel _____ (an emotion or feeling)

When _____ (describe situation observed)

Because _____ (what effect it has)

I would like/I am willing to _____ (tell what would fix the situation) [1]

You-statement: *You're always playing that bangity bang music and it's too loud!*

I-statement: *I feel irritable because I can't concentrate when the music is loud, and I have some work to do, which requires me to focus. Please turn it down.*

You-statement: *You can't go to the party.*

I- statement: *I'm afraid there will be drinking at the party, and I need to know more about who will be there. Let's talk about this a little more before we make a decision.*

You-statement: *How many times do I have to tell you to take care of your dishes?*

I-statement: *I feel overwhelmed when the clean house gets dirty so fast, then I feel angry. I would like everyone to take care of their own dishes.*

You-statement: *You never call me, what have you been up to?*

I- statement: *I miss you and would like some time with you to talk and catch up. Can we set up a time to connect?*

———

By owning our perceptions, our feelings and our needs, our communication with others becomes devoid of accusation and the inevitable response of shame, humiliation, or anger. True dialogue can begin. Building upon these communication skills, we proceeded to learn more about the CLARA method of responding to questions or verbal attacks. This is a method of communication that is effectively used when tensions are rising; at home, at work, at the Thanksgiving dinner table, or at a protest gathering. CLARA is an acronym for Centering, Listening, Affirming, Responding, and Adding Information. [2]

CENTER: As we are questioned or verbally attacked, we can internally calm ourselves and center ourselves so we can honestly be engaged in listening.

LISTEN: In any challenging interaction, listen for commonality, for a feeling or experience that we share so we can connect in some way. Try to understand what lies at the core of their question or their attack and find that common ground.

AFFIRM: Express the connection we have found as we listened or speak to what we understand as the core feeling they may be experiencing. It is finding common ground, tapping into the humanity of the other. It is important to convey the message that we are not going to attack back or hurt anyone.

RESPOND: When someone is asking a question, after listening and affirming it is important to respond by answering the question. Sometimes, the person doesn't want any response but is simply trying to fluster or attack verbally. In that case, react with respect rather than defensiveness and stay in the affirming mode.

ADD INFORMATION: This is a chance to share additional information, facts or perspective with the other person. This is possible only if there has been a connection made with the person, usually after listening and affirming with them.

Often, in a heated or tense interaction, we are prone to RESPOND, and skip over all the other aspects of the CLARA method. Or in a debate, we are listening until our opponents have their facts wrong so we can tell them the real facts and make a fool of them. Sometimes we cycle back and forth with RESPOND and ADD INFORMATION and get into a RA, RA mode. Effective communication starts with CENTERing or CALMing, and moves into the LA, LA mode of LISTENing and AFFIRMing. Once the connection of listening and affirming with another is established, then the tools of responding and adding information may be welcome, heard, and understood.

After talking about the CLARA method at the training, it was time to practice it. I found myself focusing on all these letters and the order in which they should be practiced. Feeling a bit flustered, it took me a minute to calm myself, realizing I use these skills every day in my work but I hadn't ever defined it as CLARA. It isn't a recipe to follow or a paint-by-numbers exercise. Just take a breath, and listen. I can relate to the CLARA method effectively with the words of Brené Brown, with her defining research on "Belonging." In an interview with Krista Tippett in "On Being," Brené Brown noted:

> *When you are really struggling with someone, and it is someone you're supposed to hate because of ideology or belief, move in. Get closer, get curious, ask questions. Try to connect. Find something in common. Remind yourself of that spiritual belief of inextricable connection. How am I connected to you in a way that is bigger and more primal than our politics?*[3]

It can be an exercise of risk taking and making ourselves vulnerable. But when we move in to listen and affirm, we can make a connection past our differences.

While setting up to practice this skill, we formed what is known as a "hassle line," two lines of people facing each other. Our partners across from us were tasked with making an inflammatory statement, and as responders we were to use the CLARA method, or as Brown suggests, move in.

Ready, set, go!

Line 1: *These women who are complaining of sexual harassment are ridiculous. They asked for it! Look at how they dress.*

Responder: *It sounds like you are uncomfortable.*

Line 1: *Yeah, there's a new story every day of a man being accused of "sexual misconduct." (air quotes and rolling eyes) It's just silly!*

Responder: *Sounds like you're frustrated. How is this affecting you?*

Line 1: *I don't know how to act anymore. What is sexual harassment anyway? it seems everything could be labeled as sexual harassment!*

Responder: *It sounds like it has caused some questioning of how we all behave.*

Then we switched roles and practiced another example.

Line 2: *I can't stand it! My grandson announced this weekend he was gay. How does he know he's gay? He's only 17! Maybe he'll grow out of it.*

Responder: *Sounds like it was quite a shock for you to hear that.*

Line 2: *Yeah, it was a shock! This is a sin, isn't there some camp he can go to? Maybe he'll grow out of it.*

Responder: *Is there something that worries you about his being gay?*

Line 2: *I guess I worry he'll be teased, that life will be harder for him. How does he know he's gay?*

Responder: *Sounds like you really love your grandson.*

These were relatively easy and smooth exchanges, but it isn't always this clear or kind. Often, we are confronted by angry or fearful people whose body language and verbal assaults signify an escalation in intensity, potentially to violence. This is where the skills of CLARA are most effective and needed. For instance, while at a gun control rally at the State Capitol, a man was yelling at a person holding a sign that said, "Common Sense Gun Laws NOW!" The man is leaning toward the sign holder with clenched fists. How can we use CLARA to interact?

Man yelling: *There's nothing common sense about taking away our guns! It's my right to carry a gun any time and any place I want! You namby-pambies are weak and a bunch of wimps! It's my Second Amendment right to carry a gun!*

Responder (approaching and standing between the sign holder and the man yelling): *Excuse me, hello, my name is Jonna. I can see you are very passionate about America and our rights.*

Man yelling: *You're damn right I am! And all these people want to do is take away my rights! It's my God-given right to carry my gun, and no one is going to take that away from me! It's my right to protect myself and my family and these assholes aren't gonna take that away from me!*

Responder: *I can understand you care a lot about your country and your family. We all share that passion.*

Man yelling: *Of course I care about my country and these people want to ruin it!*

Responder: *I admire your passion. I'm here today because I feel passionate too. There are many people here today who feel passionate about our country.*

Often, CLARA stays on the broken record of LA, LA; simply listening and affirming, listening and affirming. When people escalate with anger and intense emotions, they have most likely entered the "Non-Thinking Zone," and there is no capacity for reasoning. It is not the time to have a discussion about the pros and cons of an issue. Active Listening, and finding something that Affirms a common humanity, helps calm the situation. Not unless they re-enter the "Thinking Zone," will people be open to a Response or Additional Information. Until then, LA-LA is the key.

There are situations when the skills of CLARA may not work for us. Sometimes our very gender, ethnicity, or stature can make it impossible to connect with someone. We may need the support of our group or our team, or there may be another person who would be better put forward for a CLARA interaction with an irate protester. Again, Brené Brown says it best:

*I'm not going to tolerate abuse or dehumanizing language. I'm not going to have a connection with anyone who insists on diminishing my humanity. But short of that, I'm going to lean in and I'm going to stay curious.* [4]

———

Every now and then, we are witness to opportunities where we can de-escalate tense situations or interactions between two or three people. This is called Bystander Intervention, and these skills are useful when we witness harassment. It might occur anywhere, in the grocery store, at the bus stop, at work, in the classroom, at the park, or waiting for a train. As described in the Meta Peace Team Training Manual, the 4 Ds of Bystander Intervention are Direct, Distract, Delegate, and Delay. [5]

DIRECT: When we see someone being targeted, we can confront the harasser directly and let them know that what they are doing is wrong, or unacceptable. This can be risky, as the harassment may then be redirected at us, and we need to be aware when this may be uncomfortable or unsafe.

DISTRACT: When we witness harassment, approach the targeted person or the harasser and ask for the time, or for directions, pretending we are lost. Interrupt the interaction and ask unrelated questions or start singing a song at the top of your lungs. Any action that creates a distraction can help de-escalate the potential for further harassment or violence.

DELEGATE: Depending on where we are when we witness harassment, we could ask a third party to help. It could be an employee in the area, a teacher, a manager, or anyone else around. Sometimes having two or three people around to witness the harassment helps to stop it.

DELAY: If we see someone targeted with verbal harassment or non-verbal gestures such as leering, approach and ask them afterward if they are okay. At times, we may witness harassment but not be in a position to intervene safely. Asking the targeted person afterward if they are okay may help them feel less alone and can reduce their trauma. Our silence is our participation in the abuse.

After exploring these Bystander Intervention tactics, it was time to practice. The role play included an irritable mom with her child in the grocery store, with the mom getting angry at her child and verbally abusive. As a bystander, what do you do? For this role play, I happened to get the role of the mom and was instructed to yell at my "child" and start to push them. It was uncomfortable to have to perform this foreign behavior. It's not that I've never been irritated at my children, but I have not acted on that irritation with shaming, belittling or hitting my children. But that is what I was called upon to do. So I acted the part for what seemed like a very long time, eagerly awaiting the action of the bystander. But the action never came. The trainers called the role play to end and then we started debriefing or processing the role play. This is when I learned the bystander who was supposed to intervene was on the phone calling the police! We debriefed with the group for what other actions could have been taken by the bystander, noting that calling the police is not helpful in this situation. The point of Bystander Intervention is to de-escalate tense situations so that police intervention is not necessary. Examples of Bystander Intervention then could look like this:

Irritated Mom: *You brat! If I told you once, I've told you a thousand times to stop your whining and shut up! I should've left you home, you little snot! Oh, stop your crying....*

Bystander (in a singsong voice to the child): *Hey, little guy... sounds like it's been a pretty long day. May be time for a nap, eh? It won't take too much longer to get through the grocery store and then you'll be on your way!*

Or...

Bystander (in a quiet voice to the mom): *It's been a long day. I have kids too and it can be exhausting. You'll get through it.*

Another example involved riding on a bus and two men are standing too close and leering at a woman wearing a hijab. She is obviously uncomfortable with the attention. What can you do?

As bystanders, we could offer her our seat, or sit next to her, positioning our body between her and the leering men. We could start a conversation with her and completely ignore the men. We can let her know that we saw what was happening and didn't feel it was kind or appropriate and offer our presence as a witness and a support.

Bystander Intervention can often be used in one-on-one or small group settings, and can be as simple as making a short statement or asking a silly question as distraction. We may need to ask the harassed person if they need anything. It is usually not a time when the police are called. In the twenty-five years MPT has been in existence and using these skills, there has not been a time in which the police were needed or called.

———

The Meta Peace Team is often invited to regions or situations that can be a bit more intense and the tools of Third Party Nonviolent Intervention are needed. These skills are also called Unarmed Civilian Protection. The tools include: [6]

PRESENCE: Simply being a presence, a witness, and a public sign of nonviolence can often be a deterrent to violence. Many people in conflict areas note the abuse is greatly decreased when peace teams are present.

PROTECTIVE ACCOMPANIMENT: Escorting targeted people away from the area of danger or violence.

OBSERVATION/MONITORING: Using our trained sense of awareness, we can document what we see, hear and experience either by writing in a notebook, videotaping the events on a camera or phone, or voice recorders. Making this equipment visible conveys the notion that "the whole world is watching" and may deter the potential for violence.

INTERPOSITIONING: There are times when it is necessary to physically place our own bodies between the threat of violence and the targeted person. When more than one body protects someone, it is called "puppy piling."

Now that we had covered the various tools and tactics of Active Nonviolence, it was time to practice using them. Role play is a helpful method of learning the skills of Active Nonviolence. It is an opportunity to find our voice and practice the skills in a non-threatening environment and then get feedback on the interaction. It is also interesting to experience the other side of the process; the harasser or the abuser. The trainers assigned each person to a role so everyone could participate in the role play.

It was a rally of environmentalist people protesting the plan of the Water Processing Plant to take and process more water from the Great Lakes in upper Michigan. People were holding signs saying, "Save Our Water" and "Stop Corporate Greed." Two people were removed from the room and instructed to be counter-protesters, contracted and paid by the company to instigate violence and make a scene at the rally. Meanwhile, four other people were removed from the room and counseled on how to be a peace team, monitor the rally for potential problems and intervene when necessary, using the tactics we had learned that day.

I played the role of the counter-protester instigator. We were given Styrofoam batons as weapons we were to use to hit and tear at the signs of the people rallying. My protest partner and I walked into the room and heard the chants of the rally-goers. We approached and started yelling, *"What about my job? If you stop the company, I might lose my job!"* I started hitting the signs and tearing them in half. I kept screaming, *"What about my job!?!"* Then I started hitting the people holding the signs. *"What about my job?!!"* I could feel the fear and anger rising up inside me as if I could really lose my job and my livelihood, and I didn't even see the peace team people trying to stand between me and the object of my Styrofoam baton. Frightening power surged inside me because I had a weapon and they did not. Then the role play was called to an end and the debriefing discussion started.-

Each of us got to say what we experienced, how we felt, what worked, and what didn't for the peace team. This act of "harvesting" or processing the experience is an important key in learning from the role plays. I shared the experience of anger, fear, the power I felt and how invigorating it was as I used violence to deal with the insecurity I was feeling; suddenly aware for the first time why violence is the typical default behavior in our culture and maybe in humanity as a whole. It can be intoxicating. But to what end? I was so overtaken with the anger and violence within me, I hadn't even seen the people on the peace team, poorly marked in plain clothes rather than the usual yellow vests of MPT. Apparently, they were trying to talk to me, using their best efforts at the CLARA method, but I wasn't hearing any of it. The peace team eventually tried to separate the target of my anger, when the role play was called to an end. Perhaps if the bright yellow color and the words "PEACE TEAM" were in front of me, I would have been distracted long enough to calm down. It was an eye-opening experience. And it was humbling.

The trainers then demonstrated other strategies which would have worked in such an escalation to violence from someone who had obviously entered the Non-Thinking Zone. Peter, the trainer, stood with his back to me, the aggressor, to position himself between me and my target. Other members of the peace team could then swiftly escort the targets away from the potential danger. There are many tools to use in the nonviolent toolbox, and as the situation morphs further into tension, quick thinking is needed to swap tools.

The next role play included all the participants as well. The setting was a walkway leading from a place where a white nationalist had just finished speaking. As participants leave, they see people holding "Black Lives Matter" signs and decide to harass the protesters. Then, members of Antifa (an anti-fascist group open to using violence) approach the white nationalists and get in their faces, begging for a fight. As tensions rise, the peace team is to approach the group and intervene. The members of the peace team realize they need to actually protect the white nationalists, so they position their bodies between them and the Antifa members and try to accompany the white nationalists away from the group. The role play was called to an end. And then, standing in our spots, we processed.

Being part of a peace team means not taking sides. It means we use our tactics to keep people safe, even people with whom we do not agree. We are present to allow people with varying ideas and thoughts to come together and interact, perhaps angrily, but in a nonviolent way. Our goal isn't to shut down dissent and protest, but to de-escalate the climate when it gets so heated it may turn violent. No one is heard and nothing is accomplished once it gets to the violence. Active Nonviolence does not intend to end conflict, or propose a world where there is no conflict. Rather, Active Nonviolence recognizes that we face conflict all through our lives. Recognizing conflict is the first step toward "moving in," and honoring our shared humanity. We can move *through* the conflict in a nonviolent way.

> *Peace does not mean the absence of conflicts; differences will always be there. Peace means solving these differences through peaceful means; through dialogue, education, knowledge, and through humane ways. Dalai Lama XIV* [7]

We returned to our seats after practicing the skills of de-escalation and Active Nonviolence, feeling invigorated and energized, but overwhelmed with the grayness and the realities of this work.

I sat thinking that the work of nonviolence is harder than violence. It is easy to throw a punch, wield a club, shoot a gun, or drop a bomb. Anyone can do that. But the work of nonviolence takes patience, creativity and commitment, using our brains, our heart and our bodies. We are all called to grow in this life in whatever way we can; physically, emotionally, mentally, and spiritually. It was becoming clearer to me, the active nonviolent way of approaching conflict is a transcendent challenge for human beings, but one I wanted to pursue and understand personally. We humans can be better than we are; kinder to each other than we are; listen more carefully to each other than we do; take better care of each other and the earth than we have. But the narrative needs to change. So much of what we see on the news or experience in our lives celebrates the opposite, and we are told these hurtful messages over and over so they are normalized. We can change the narrative to include and raise the awareness of the strength involved in nonviolence. True courage lies here.

# ACKNOWLEDGMENTS

I think of gratitude as a heart full of love. Mine is overflowing as I look back at the process of writing this book and bringing it to your hands. I am especially grateful to Peter Dougherty; for his honesty, his consistency, and his eagerness to share his story. And for Mary Hanna, Kim Redigan, Sheri Wander, Elliott Adams, Dwight Washington, Katie Ames, Laura Ray, Barbara Harvey, Kathleen Hernandez, Linda Sartor, Amy Schneidhorst, and Pat Thornburg, who opened their calendars and their hearts to share their experiences with nonviolence, and the effect Meta Peace Team has had in their lives. I appreciate Kerry Shaffer for sharing information about Jasiu Milanowski as the Meta Peace Team would not be what it is today without him. Thank you for allowing me to put your stories into prose and communicate to the world that peace is possible. You are living that effort every day.

Friends are the stars that help me appreciate the night sky. I am grateful to have many, but those listed here were brave enough to read my various renditions and give thoughtful feedback; Justine Peters, Diane Strachan, Rocky Beckett, Peter Dougherty, LaRay Bonney, Coleen Moyerbralien, Robert Darios, Chris Morland, Joanne Thomas, Nancy Schertzing and Pat Cavanaugh. Thank you for your excitement and your support. For her incredible skill in making my website a reality, I am forever grateful to Theresa

Goodreau. And thank you, Mary Fairgrieve, for suggesting Mission Point Press. It was an amazing match and one I would not have found without you.

It felt like putting the last puzzle piece into place when I spoke with the people at Mission Point Press. They have been professional and supportive from the start. Owner Doug Weaver instructed me through the process and paired me with an ideal editor, Gary Marx. His clarifying questions, active listening skills and excellent editing abilities were exactly what I needed to feel confident about the finished product. Designer Heather Shaw worked her magic to turn my manuscript into this book. Marketing specialist Jodee Taylor expertly guided me through unfamiliar waters. I could not have picked a better team for this adventure.

I am lucky enough to have family who love me, although we don't always land on the same side of issues. Thank you for listening; Del and Joanne Thomas, Jim and Marie Thomas, Tim Thomas and Shellie Rich, Theresa and Cornell Goodreau, LaRay and Bill Bonnie, Bobbiejo Ellens and Raymond Beckett and my incredible nieces and nephews.

I am honored to be called 'mom' by Aaron Beckett and Elizabeth Beckett. Thank you for teaching me every day, and showing me what joy looks like. My life feels whole because of you.

I am a stone being polished as I celebrate life with my husband, Rocky Ray Beckett. Traveling side by side, learning and growing together, tumbling down sometimes, then getting back up to rub out the rough edges, I am eternally grateful for our 'You-Me-Us.' Thank you for loving me and letting me love you.

Mostly, I thank the reader. For your attention, your interest, and especially your courage. Nonviolence is possible because of you.

Sincerely,
*Julie Thomas-Beckett*

*Photo by Elizabeth Beckett*
*East Lansing, MI*
*March 2020*

# ABOUT THE AUTHOR

Julie Thomas-Beckett feels acutely aware of a huge Circle of Concern, but has found writing this book as a way to stay focused on her Circle of Influence. She has participated on Domestic Peace Teams and is a trainer for the Meta Peace Team. She practices the skills of active listening in her everyday life as a Nurse Practitioner at her Family Practice in East Lansing, MI. She is a wife, a mom, a daughter, a teacher, a mentor, a rebel. She lives in East Lansing with her husband and their cute little dog, named Leo. This is her first book. Check out her blog at juliethomasbeckett.com

# REFERENCES

**Introduction**

1.   The Bill of Rights in the Constitution of the United States
2.   *The Ann Arbor News*, online publication. Article by Ryan Stanton 10-31-2013
3.   *The Ann Arbor News*, online publication. Article by Martin Slagter 6-24-2016
4.   *The Ann Arbor News*, online. Article by Martin Slagter 6-24-2016
5.   Fowles, John (1993). *The Aristos*, Pan Books Limited, pp.9-10
6.   Attributed to Native American legends, no specific author found

**Chapter One**

1.   Jamnalal Bajaj International Gandhi Award 2009, on 11-4-2009 in Mumbai, India
2.   Interview with Peter Dougherty 7-7-2017
3.   Interview with Peter Dougherty 6-30-2017
4.   Interview with Peter Dougherty 7-7-2017
5.   "Gandhi: An Introduction" by Jasiu Milanowski, Grand Rapids peace team, Grand Rapids, MI. 2002
6.   "Gandhi: An Introduction" by Jasiu Milanowski, Grand Rapids peace team, Grand Rapids, MI. 2002 p.2

7.  Nagler, Michael, N. (2014). *The Nonviolent Handbook*. Berrett-Koehler Publishing, San Francisco, CA.
8.  Nagler, Michael, N. (2014). *The Nonviolent Handbook*. Berrett-Koehler Publishing, San Francisco, CA. p.12
9.  "Gandhi: An Introduction" by Jasiu Milanowski, Grand Rapids peace team, Grand Rapids, MI. 2002 p.6
10. Interview with Peter Dougherty 7-7-2017
11. Interview with Peter Dougherty 7-7-2017
12. Michigan/Meta Peace Team Nonviolence Training and Skills Sharing Trainers' Handbook. p.7
13. Michigan/Meta Peace Team Nonviolence Training and Skills Sharing Trainers' Handbook. p.11
14. Interview with Peter Dougherty 8-1-2017

## Chapter Two

1.  Interview with Peter Dougherty 8-1-2017
2.  Interview with Peter Dougherty 8-1-2017
3.  Wild Clearing Video Interview of Jasiu Milanowski
4.  *The Holland Sentinal*, 9-17-2017
5.  Interview with Peter Dougherty 7-14-2017
6.  Nagler, Michael, N. (2014). *The Nonviolent Handbook*. Berrett-Koehler Publishing, San Francisco, CA. p.14
7.  Interview with Peter Dougherty 10-24-2018
8.  Interview with Peter Dougherty 10-24-2018

## Chapter Three

1.  Interview with Mary Hanna 8-22-2017
2.  Interview with Mary Hanna 8-22-2017

3.  Spoken at the Meta Peace Team Development Retreat by Mary Hanna at the St. Augustine Center in Oxford, MI  12-2-2018
4.  Interview with Mary Hanna 8-22-2017
5.  Chenoweth, E., & Stephan, M.J. (2011). *Why Civil Resistance Works: The Strategic Logic of Nonviolent Conflict*. Columbia University Press, New York p.17
6.  Chenoweth, E., & Stephan, M.J. (2011). *Why Civil Resistance Works: The Strategic Logic of Nonviolent Conflict*. Columbia University Press, New York. p.9
7.  Chenoweth, E., & Stephan, M.J. (2011). *Why Civil Resistance Works: The Strategic Logic of Nonviolent Conflict*. Columbia University Press, New York.  p.10
8.  Chenoweth, E., & Stephan, M.J. (2011). *Why Civil Resistance Works: The Strategic Logic of Nonviolent Conflict*. Columbia University Press, New York.  p.10
9.  Chenoweth, E., & Stephan, M.J. (2011). *Why Civil Resistance Works: The Strategic Logic of Nonviolent Conflict*. Columbia University Press, New York. p.29
10. Interview with Mary Hanna 8-22-2017
11. Interview with Mary Hanna 8-22-2017
12. Interview with Mary Hanna 8-22-2017
13. Interview with Mary Hanna 8-22-2017
14. Interview with Mary Hanna 8-22-2017

## Chapter Four

1.  Interview with Kim Redigan 1-14-2018
2.  Interview with Kim Redigan 1-14-2018
3.  Interview with Kim Redigan 1-14-2018
4.  Interview with Kim Redigan 1-14-2018
5.  Interview with Kim Redigan 1-14-2018
6.  Interview with Kim Redigan 1-14-2018

7.  Boyle, Father Gregory, (2017). *Barking to the Choir*. Simon and Schuster, New York, NY. p.201.
8.  Interview with Kim Redigan 1-18-2019
9.  Interview with Kim Redigan 1-18-2019
10. Interview with Kim Redigan 1-14-2018
11. Interview with Kim Redigan 1-14-2018

## Chapter Five

1.  Interview with Sheri Wander, 11-7-2018
2.  Frye, Marilyn (1983). "The Politics of Reality; Essays in Feminist Theory" The Crossing Press, Trumansburg, New York.
3.  Frye, Marilyn (1983). "The Politics of Reality; Essays in Feminist Theory" The Crossing Press, Trumansburg, New York.
4.  Interview with Sheri Wander, 11-7-2018
5.  Interview with Sheri Wander 11-7-2018
6.  Interview with Sheri Wander 11-7-2018
7.  Interview with Sheri Wander 11-7-2018
8.  Democracy Now interview of Danielle Sered by Amy Goodman 3-14-2019
9.  Interview with Sheri Wander 11-7-2018
10. Interview with Sheri Wander 11-7-2018
11. Interview with Sheri Wander 2-10-2018
12. Interview with Sheri Wander 2-10-2018
13. Interview with Sheri Wander 11-7-2018
14. Interview with Sheri Wander 11-7-2018

## Chapter Six

1.  Interview with Peter Dougherty 7-14-2017
2.  Interview with Peter Dougherty 7-14-2017
3.  Interview with Peter Dougherty 7-14-2017

4. Interview with Elliott Adams 9-13-2017

5. Interview with Elliott Adams 9-13-2017

6. Interview with Elliott Adams 9-13-2017

7. Interview with Elliott Adams 9-13-2017

8. Whyte, David. (2014). *Consolations*. Many River Press, Langley, WA. p.39

9. Interview with Elliott Adams 9-13-2017

10. Interview with Elliott Adams 9-13-2017

11. Interview with Elliott Adams 9-13-2017

12. Interview with Elliott Adams 9-20-2017

13. Interview with Elliott Adams 9-20-2017

14. Interview with Elliott Adams 9-20-2017

15. Interview with Elliott Adams 9-20-2017

## Chapter Seven

1. Interview with Mary Hanna 8-22-2017

2. Interview with Mary Hanna 8-22-2017

3. Interview with Mary Hanna 8-22-2017

4. Interview with Mary Hanna 8-22-2017

5. Interview with Kim Redigan 1-18-2019

6. Interview with Kim Redigan 1-18-2019

7. Interview with Kim Redigan 1-14-2018

8. Interview with Kim Redigan 1-14-2018

9. Interview with Kim Redigan 1-14-2018

10. Interview with Barbara Harvey 2-12-2019

11. Interview with Barbara Harvey 2-12-2019

12. Interview with Barbara Harvey 2-12-2019

13. Sartor, L. (2018). *Turning Fear Into Power: How I Confronted the War on Terror*. Cune Press, Seattle, WA

14. Sartor, L. (2018). *Turning Fear Into Power: How I Confronted the War on Terror*. Cune Press, Seattle, WA p.30

15. Sartor, L. (2018). *Turning Fear Into Power: How I Confronted the War on Terror*. Cune Press, Seattle, WA pp.24-25
16. Sartor, L. (2018). *Turning Fear Into Power: How I Confronted the War on Terror*. Cune Press, Seattle, WA p.41
17. Sartor, L. (2018). *Turning Fear Into Power: How I Confronted the War on Terror*. Cune Press, Seattle, WA p. 45
18. Sartor, L. (2018). *Turning Fear Into Power: How I Confronted the War on Terror*. Cune Press, Seattle, WA pp.53-54
19. Sartor, L. (2018). *Turning Fear Into Power: How I Confronted the War on Terror*. Cune Press, Seattle, WA p.56.
20. Interview with Linda Sartor 9-20-2018
21. Interview with Linda Sartor 9-20-2018
22. Sartor, L. (2018). *Turning Fear Into Power: How I Confronted the War on Terror*. Cune Press, Seattle, WA p.13

## Chapter Eight

1. Interview with Kathleen Hernandez 3-24-2019
2. Interview with Pat Thornburg 3-21-2019
3. Interview with Kathleen Hernandez 3-24-2019
4. Interview with Pat Thornburg 3-21-2019
5. Interview with Kathleen Hernandez 3-24-2019
6. Interview with Kim Redigan 3-14-2019
7. Interview with Mary Hanna 3-10-2019
8. Interview with Kim Redigan 3-14-2019
9. Interview with Mary Hanna 3-10-2019
10. Interview with Amy Schneidhorst 3-16-2019
11. Interview with Amy Schneidhorst 3-16-2019
12. Interview with Mary Hanna 3-10-2019
13. King James Bible; Book of Matthew 25:35
14. Interview with Kim Redigan 3-14-2019
15. Interview with Kathleen Hernandez 3-24-2019

16. Interview with Pat Thornburg 3-21-2019
17. Interview with Kim Redigan 3-14-2019
18. Interview with Mary Hanna 3-10-2019

## Chapter Nine

1. Dwight Washington at MPT Bystander Intervention Training, Lansing Community College, 1-31-2020
2. Interview with Dwight Washington 10-17-2017
3. Interview with Dwight Washington 10-17-2017
4. Interview with Dwight Washington 10-17-2017
5. Interview with Mary Ellen Jeffreys 2-6-2019
6. Interview with Dwight Washington 10-17-2017
7. Nagler, Michael. (2014). *The Nonviolent Handbook*. Berrett-Koehler Publishing, Inc, San Francisco, CA. p.6
8. Interview with Laura M. Ray 1-28-2019
9. "Story Corps" NPR, started by David Isay. Story presented on National Public Radio on 4-12-2019
10. Interview with Nancy Schertzing 3-16-2019
11. Jewish Voice for Peace website
12. Jewish Voice for Peace website
13. Harvey, Barbara. Remarks for the Women's March in Detroit, MI 1-19-2019.
14. Interview with Barbara Harvey 2-12-2019
15. Rosenberg, Marshall B. (2015). *Nonviolent Communication: A Language of Life*. Puddle Dancer Press
16. Interview with Katie Ames 1-30-2019
17. Interview with Katie Ames 1-30-2019
18. Interview with Katie Ames 1-30-2019
19. Interview with Katie Ames 1-30-2019

## Conclusion

1. Quote from Rachel Naomi Remen, MD, in her interview with Krista Tippett in "On Being." Originally aired on 8-11-2005, updated 11-22-2018
2. Remen, Rachel Naomi, (1996). Kitchen Table Wisdom. The Berkley Publishing Company, New York, NY. pp.114-118
3. Bush, George H.W. in his speech accepting the presidential nomination at the 1988 Republican National Convention in New Orleans, Louisiana, and at his Inaugural Address, 1989
4. Nagler, Michael N. (2014). *The Nonviolent Handbook*, Berrett-Koelher Publishing, San Francisco, CA. p.61
5. Interview with Donna Kaplowitz 2-9-2019
6. Powers, Chet (stage name Dino Valenti) 1964, song "Get Together"

## Appendix

1. Meta Peace Team Violence De-escalation Skills Training Manual p.7
2. Meta Peace Team Violence De-escalation Skills Training Manual pp.8-9
3. "On Being" interview with Brené Brown and Krista Tippett
4. "On Being" interview with Brené Brown and Krista Tippett
5. Meta Peace Team Violence De-escalation Skills Training Manual p.13
6. Liz Walters in the Meta Peace Team Violence De-escalation Skills Training Manual p.15
7. Dalai Lama XIV in the Meta Peace Team Violence De-escalation Skills Training Manual p.10